The Batsford Guide to Racing Cars

**Compiled by
Denis Jenkinson**

**B.T. Batsford Ltd
London**

© Denis Jenkinson 1978

First published 1978

Based on the original publication *The Racing Car Pocketbook*, 1962

ISBN 0 7134 1273 9

Filmset by Servis Filmsetting Limited, Manchester
Printed in Great Britain by Butler & Tanner Ltd, Frome
for the publishers B.T. Batsford Limited
4 Fitzhardinge Street, London W1H 0AH

Contents

	Page		Page
Acknowledgment	5	Cosworth 4-W-D	62
Introduction	6	Coyote	63
		Cromard Special	64
AFM	8	Crosslé	65
AJB	9	CTA-Arsenal	66
Alfa Romeo	10	Daf	67
Allard	14	DB	68
Alta	15	Delahaye	69
Amon-Dalton	17	Derby Maserati	70
Appleton Special	18	Derby-Miller	71
Arzani-Volpini	19	Derrington Francis	72
Aston Martin	20	De Tomaso	73
ATS	22	Dommartin	74
Austin	23	Duesenberg	75
Auto Union	25	Eagle	76
Barnato-Hassan	27	Elva	78
BHW	29	Emeryson Special	79
BMW	30	Ensign	81
Bolster Special	31	ERA	83
Brabham	32	ERA-Delage	84
BRM	35	Ferguson	85
Brooke Special	39	Ferrari	87
BRP	40	Fittipaldi	92
Bugatti	41	Ford	93
Challenger	45	Frazer Nash	94
Challenger-1	46	Freikaiserwagon	96
Chevron	47	Fuzzi	97
Chrysler	48	Gilby	99
Cisitalia	49	Goldenrod	100
Connaught	51	Gordini	100
Connew	52	Hesketh	102
Cooper-Alta	53	Hill	104
Cooper-Alta Special	54	Honda	105
Cooper-Bristol	55	Hotchkiss	108
Cooper-Bristol (rear-engined)	56	HRG	108
		HWM	109
Cooper-Climax	57	Invicta	111
Cooper-ERA	59	Kieft	112
Cooper-Maserati	60	Kojima	113
Cooper-Norton	61	Kurtis	114

	Page		Page
Lancia	115	Ralt	163
Lancia-Ferrari	116	Renault	164
Lec	117	Riley	165
Lightweight Special	118	Rover	167
Ligier	119	RRA	168
Lister-Climax	120	Sacha-Gordine	169
Lola	121	Scarab	170
Lotus	123	SEFAC	171
Maki	128	Shadow	172
Maserati	128	Squire	174
Maserati-Milan	132	Stanguellini	174
Maserati-Platé	133	STP-Turbocar	175
March	134	Surtees	176
Martini	137	Talbot	178
Matra	138	Talbot-Lago	179
Matra-Cosworth	139	Tecno	180
Maybach Special	140	Tec-Mec	182
McLaren	141	Terrapin	183
McNamara	144	Thinwall Special	184
Mercédès-Benz	145	Trojan	185
MG	148	Trossi-Monaco	186
Multi-Union	150	Tyrrell	187
Napier-Railton	151	Vale Special	191
Novi-Ferguson	153	Vanwall	192
Novi-Special	154	Vauxhall-Villiers	193
OBM	154	Veritas	194
Osca	155	Watson	195
Parnelli	157	Williams	196
Penske	158	Wolf	198
Porsche	159	Zoller	199
Railton-Mobil Special	161		

Acknowledgment

The Author is most grateful to the following people for the loan of photographs and for their permission to reproduce them here: John Bolster, Geoffrey Goddard, Guy Griffiths, Anthony Harding, David Hodges, J.H. Horsman, F. Wilson McComb, Cyril Posthumus, Alan Staniforth, and to the Indianapolis Motor Speedway.

Thanks are due also to the following organisations: Autosport, BMW Gmbh, Copersucar, Citicorp, Chevron Cars, Elf, Embassy, Ford Motor Co., Gitanes, Keystone Press Agency, Marlboro, Martini Rossi, Matra, Phipps Photographic, STP, Sunoco, UOP, Vandervell Products and Walter Wolf Racing.

The remainder of the photographs are taken from the Author's own collection.

Introduction

The original version of this book, published in 1962, covered racing cars from the dawn of motoring to the year of publication. This second edition is slightly altered in that it deals with racing cars from the end of the Vintage period to the present day, the cars of the earlier times being dealt with in another volume.

In compiling this second edition I made a number of decisions which the reader will have to accept for better or for worse. The term 'racing car' I restricted to single-seater cars built for racing or record breaking and have taken Grand Prix or Formula 1 cars as my basis. All told I gathered together a list of some 269 different makes of single-seater racing car and obviously it was impossible to incorporate tham all in a reference book of this size. If I had done so it would have become a book suitable only for an unlimited pocket. In consequence I have settled for 137 makes, my choice being dictated by numerous things such as importance in the world motor racing scene, representatives of various branches of motor racing, interesting one-off special cars, personal likes and so on. In the past 20 years the art of building racing cars has undergone a vast change and there is now so much knowledge available that building a racing car presents few problems—the problems arise in building a successful racing car. This knowledge was started principally by small firms like Cooper, Lotus and Lola and their task was made easier by the growth of specialist engine and transmission firms. If Coventry-Climax, Ford, BMC and Cosworth had not produced production racing engines, it is doubtful whether the small firms would have got very far and we might have been left with a situation where a racing car had to be built in its entirety by the manufacturer, as Ferrari and BRM do today.

Although the art of special building is as old as motor racing, and examples are cited of such cars from the '30s, using proprietary engines in a home-made chassis, they were usually one-off cars, for the enjoyment of the constructor. With the advent of Formula 3 and 500-cc racing after the 1939–45 war Cooper set the ball rolling for special building in quantity for sale, with Cooper-JAP, Cooper-Norton and Cooper-Bristol cars, and since then the activity has snowballed and become the normal state of affairs, racing-car manufacturers who build their own engines being a rarity. Other great assets to the present business of commercial special building were the advent of the welded tubular space-frame, and later, the rivetted aluminium monocoque chassis. The introduction of the oxy-acetylene welding plant and the pop-rivetting gun have done more for motor racing than it would be possible to illustrate.

In Formula Junior of 1959–63 there were some 88 different manufacturers, and this proliferation has moved into the present Formula Ford; in one

FF event in 1976 there were 27 different makes. Clearly it was impossible to feature all these in a *Guide*, and to a lesser degree this problem exists with almost every racing Formula, so examples have been taken at random, with a slight bias to personal preference, tinged with valour. If your favourite Formula Ford or Formula 3 car is not included I can only apologize for having different taste. Nearly all Formula 1 cars are featured as this is the category that racing-car manufacturers are all aiming for. Examples are given of both success and failure to illustrate that it is not an easy path to the top.

Many firms, such as Lola, Lotus, Ferrari and so on carried on a sports-car racing programme as well as a single-seater programme, but these are not mentioned as it would confuse the issue and diversify the intent of this *Guide*.

Denis Jenkinson

Crondall, Hampshire 1978

AFM   Germany

In view of the chaos in Germany after the 1939–45 war, motor-racing enthusiasts took things into their own hands. One such enthusiast was Alex von Falkenhausen, who was connected with the BMW factory at Munich. In a small private workshop he set about developing a pre-war 328 BMW sports car into a single-seater racing car for the rather haphazard racing held in Germany in those early revival days. Falkenhausen did a great deal of development on the 328 engine, running it on alcohol fuel, and driven notably by Hans Stuck the car made quite a name for itself, under the title AFM, standing for Alex von Falkenhausen Motorenbau. Several examples were built during those early days, the basis being a 328 sports car, and some sports AFMs were also built, lighter and more compact than the 328 BMW. The single-seaters were developed with a tubular space-frame and de Dion rear-axle layout.

In 1950 Falkenhausen began to move back to the BMW factory as an engineer, but before abandoning his AFM firm he installed a 4-ohc V8 engine, designed by Richard Küchen, into his works car. This was a 2-litre unit for the current Formula 2 and it was raced extensively by Stuck and though it was incredibly fast and accelerative it lacked reliability. Before it was fully developed Falkenhausen closed down AFM as work at BMW was occupying all his time.

The works car had the V8 engine replaced by a 2-litre Bristol engine when imported into England where it was used in VSCC Historic racing until a very bad accident almost destroyed it.

Hans Stuck driving the V8 AFM 2-litre on the Bremgarten circuit in 1950

Year: 1950
Model: Formula 2
Engine: Küchen
Number of cylinders: 8 in-vee
Bore and Stroke: 67·3 × 70 mm
Capacity: 1993 cc
Valves: Inclined overhead. 4 ohcs
Induction: Eight down-draught carburettors
Wheelbase: 8 ft 0 in
Forward Speeds: 4
Front Suspension: Independent by double wishbones and coil springs
Rear Suspension: de Dion with torsion bars
Chassis Frame: Tubular
Maximum Speed: 145 mph

AJB England

Designed and built by Archie Butterworth, the AJB was primarily a sprint and hill-climb car, though it did do some circuit racing and actually ran in the 1950 International Trophy at Silverstone. Butterworth started on the project in 1948 and in 1949 he made FTD at the Brighton Speed Trials, as well as recording impressive acceleration times at many other venues. The point about Archie's car was that it used 4-wheel-drive as he wished to prove this form of transmission was the best.

Archie Butterworth in action at Silverstone with his 4-wheel-drive creation

He used an ex-Army Jeep chassis and axles, boxed the side members for more rigidity, located the axles more positively and installed a German Army Steyr V8 engine, of Austrian manufacture, this being an air-cooled unit of 3·7 litres with individual motor-cycle-type cylinder barrels and over-head valves operated by pushrods. By making new barrels and pistons the bore was increased from 79 to 87·5 mm, increasing the capacity to $4\frac{1}{2}$ litres, and the compression was raised to 14:1. A new camshaft was made and eight Amal carburettors were fitted, the improvements putting the power output up to nearly 250 bhp. The Steyr 3-speed gearbox was retained and behind this was fitted a train of gears, stepping the drive sideways, from which propellor shafts ran fore and aft to the rather heavy Jeep axles.

A sketchy bodywork covered the mechanism and the sight of the bearded Butterworth literally cornering on the two outside wheels, seemingly unconcerned, with the air-cooled cylinders sticking out of each side of the bonnet, accompanied by the shattering noise of the Steyr V8, was something that made weak people stagger away from the course. Eventually Archie up-ended the car rather seriously at Shelsey Walsh injuring himself and he forthwith retired from competitions and got on with engineering problems in his small experimental workshop. The car was sold to Bill Milliken of the

Cornell Aeronautical Laboratory in Buffalo, USA, where it was used for some research into 4-wheel-drive as well as being used in hill-climbs. He retains the car to this day.

Year: 1949
Model: 4-W-D
Engine: Steyr
Number of cylinders: 8 in-vee, air-cooled
Bore and Stroke: 87·5 × 92 mm
Capacity: 4425 cc
Valves: Inclined overhead with pushrods

Induction: Eight Amal carburettors
Wheelbase: 7 ft 6 in
Forward Speeds: 3
Front and Rear Suspension: Semi-elliptic leaf springs
Chassis Frame: Boxed channel-section
Maximum Speed: 150 mph

Alfa Romeo
Italy

The name of Alfa Romeo is one that is always connected with motor racing, and though the origins go back to 1906 it was 1909 when the 'Societa Anonima Lombarda Fabbrica Automobili' (ALFA) was formed. The following year the firm raced with modified production cars in the Targa Florio, and in 1914 they built a GP car, with 4-cylinder engine of 100×143 mm—$4\frac{1}{2}$ litres—with a top speed of 90 mph. Ing. Nicola Romeo took over the factory, the firm being known as 'Societa Anonima Italiana Ing. Nicola Romeo' and in 1918 the name changed to Alfa Romeo. In 1919 they were back in racing with the 1914 GP $4\frac{1}{2}$-litre cars and formed a team consisting of Ugo Sivocci, Enzo Ferrari, Giuseppe Campari and Antonio Ascari. The first post-war GP car was produced in 1923, being the P1—supercharged 6-cylinder. Unfortunately Sivocci was killed in one of the cars while practising for the Italian GP, and the rest of the team were withdrawn.

Louis Chiron in a 1935 'monoposto' at the Monaco GP

Vittorio Jano joined the firm, and assisted by Luigi Bazzi, a new team of cars was built for 1924. These were 8-cylinder supercharged 2-litre cars, giving 140 bhp at 5400 rpm. Known as the P2 they won their first race. They also won the French GP and finished 1-2-3-4 in the Italian GP. In 1925 the P2 team swept the GP board, won the Manufacturers' Championship and Alfa Romeo added the laurel wreath surround to their existing badge.

The bi-motore Alfa Romeo being driven to 2nd place in the 1935 Avusrennen by Louis Chiron

For 1926 Alfa Romeo withdrew from GP racing, starting again in 1929–30 with the P2 cars when racing was to *Formule Libre*. In 1931 they built an entirely new car which was to start a successful line. This was the 8C, a supercharged 8-cylinder of 2·3 litres, using a central train of gears between cylinders 4 and 5 driving two ohcs. GP racing was for cars of 2-seater width and the 8C or 'Monza', as it became known unofficially, was used for GP racing as well as sports-car racing. The same year the firm experimented unsuccessfully with the Tipo A, which had two 6-cylinder sports engines of 1750 cc mounted side-by-side. It caused the death of Luigi Arcangeli, one of the works drivers, and although a Tipo A won the 1931 Pescara race they were finally abandoned. The new car was the Tipo B, which was one of the most successful racing cars. Better known as the 'monoposto', this Alfa Romeo became one of the classic Grand cars of all time. The engine was a supercharged 8-cylinder of 2·6-litres capacity, using the central gear drive to the ohcs, and with twin superchargers it gave 180 bhp at 5400 rpm. The chassis was narrow with unusual rear-axle layout, using two propeller shafts diverging from behind the gearbox, where the differential was mounted, to two crown-wheel-and-pinion assemblies. This was the European GP car of single-seater form that set a trend and was most successful in 1932–33. For the new Formula in 1934 it needed little modification, but by now Alfa Romeo had withdrawn from racing and the Scuderia Ferrari under the leadership of Enzo Ferrari was doing all the official racing for the factory.

The 1934 Tipo B 'monoposto' is wrongly called the P3 by some people who think it followed the successful 1924 cars, whereas it actually followed on from the less successful 1931 Tipo A 'twin-six'. An increase in cylinder bore gave it a capacity of 2·9 litres and in 1935 it was developed with Dubonnet independent suspension at the front and reversed quarter-elliptic springs at the rear; the capacity was further increased to 3·2 litres. In this year Ferrari and Bazzi built two fantastic machines for *Formule Libre* races called 'Bi-motore'. As the name suggests, they had two engines, fore and aft of the driver, both driving the rear wheels. One car had two 2·9-litre Tipo B engines and the other had the later 3·2-litre engines. They were incredibly fast, the larger-engined car setting records at just over 200 mph but were too hard on their tyres to be successful in racing. They managed 2nd at Avus and 4th and 5th at Tripoli.

In 1936 a new 4-litre V12 was used, later enlarged to $4\frac{1}{2}$ litres and also a similar chassis using a 3·8-litre 8-cylinder and these two models were the mainstay of the Scuderia Ferrari racing throughout the season. For the new Formula in 1938 Alfa Romeo restarted their own racing department under the name of 'Alfa Corse', and they produced three models, all of 3-litres capacity—an 8-cylinder, a 12-cylinder and a 16-cylinder—but none of them was highly successful and the firm turned its attention to 'voiturette' racing. Jano's assistant, Gioacchino Columbo, designed a $1\frac{1}{2}$-litre 8-cylinder engine that was virtually half of the GP 16-cylinder engine, with identical bore and stroke of 58×70 mm. This was put into a chassis that was a scaled-down GP car, and the famous Tipo 158 'Alfetta' was born. It went from strength to strength during 1939 and 1940 and after the war was brought out again in 1946 to set the standard for the post-war Formula in 1947. It was unapproachable in 1947 and 1948 and the team was withdrawn for 1949 as there was little opposition, but they restarted in 1950 with the same basic cars slightly modified and called the Tipo 159. It was not until the middle of the 1951 season that the Tipo 158/9 Alfa Romeo was soundly beaten, by which time the 8-cylinder $1\frac{1}{2}$-litre engine had been developed from 170 bhp to over 380 bhp.

The 1951 version of the Tipo 159 was the last Alfa Romeo single-seater racing car to be built, as the firm withdrew at the end of that season. The swansong of the '159' was at Monza when Farina took over the last remaining car of the team and drove flat-out in an attempt to catch the leaders. The scream of that supercharged engine running continuously to 9000 rpm in a vain attempt to win remains as one of the landmarks of GP racing. Why the engine did not fly apart as the rest of the team's had done we shall never know, but it gained 3rd place. The season ended with a win in Spain and then the '159' retired.

Although Alfa Romeo stopped GP racing they did continue in sports-car racing, and in recent years came to an arrangement with British chassis-builders to use V8 and flat-12 Alfa Romeo engines in Formula 1 cars, described elsewhere in this book. Most successful of these has been the association with Brabham cars, the Brabham-Alfa Romeo flat-12 becoming virtually an Alfa Romeo Formula 1 car.

Dr. Farina in an Alfa Romeo Tipo 159 at Silverstone in 1951

Year: 1934
Model: Tipo B
Engine: Alfa Romeo
Number of cylinders: 8 in-line
Bore and Stroke: 68 × 100 mm
Capacity: 2905 cc
Valves: Inclined overhead with two ohcs
Induction: Twin Roots superchargers
Wheelbase: 8 ft 8⅝ in
Forward Speeds: 3
Front Suspension: Semi-elliptic leaf springs
Rear Suspension: Semi-elliptic leaf springs with divided prop-shaft axle
Chassis Frame: Channel-section
Maximum Speed: 145 mph

Year: 1937
Model: 12C-36
Engine: Alfa Romeo
Number of cylinders: 12 in-vee
Bore and Stroke: 72 × 92 mm
Capacity: 4495 cc
Valves: Inclined overhead with four ohcs
Induction: Twin Roots superchargers
Wheelbase: 9 ft 2 in
Forward Speeds: 4
Front Suspension: Independent by trailing arms and oil immersed coil springs
Rear Suspension: Independent by swing axles
Chassis Frame: Channel-section
Maximum Speed: 170 mph

Year: 1938/51
Model: Tipo 158/159
Engine: Alfa Romeo
Number of cylinders: 8 in-line
Bore and Stroke: 58 × 70 mm
Capacity: 1479 cc
Valves: Inclined overhead with two ohcs
Induction: Two-stage Roots supercharging
Wheelbase: 8 ft 2½ in
Forward Speeds: 4
Front Suspension: Independent by trailing arms and transverse leaf spring
Rear Suspension: Independent by swing axles and transverse leaf spring
Chassis Frame: Tubular
Maximum Speed: 180 mph

13

Allard England

Sydney Allard branched out from making sports cars with Ford V8 engines into the racing sphere in 1947, when he built a special sprint and hill-climb car, using an air-cooled V8 Steyr military engine. The chassis was basically the same as his sports cars, with swing axle i.f.s. by a split Ford beam and a rigid Ford rear axle with transverse leaf spring, but this was soon replaced by a de Dion rear axle. The Steyr engine underwent a lot of development with new high-compression pistons, barrels with increased bore, new heads and eight carburettors. The result was a very light vehicle that won the RAC Hill-climb Championship in 1949.

After a pause from sprints and hill-climbs Allard returned in 1959 with a vast and complicated 4-wheel-drive machine containing two Steyr engines, mounted side-by-side, but this was an abortive attempt and was quickly abandoned. In 1961 he built an American style 'Dragster' of the sling-shot type, wherein the driver sits behind the rear axle with his legs passing forward over it. A tubular frame had a simple Ford-type axle at the front, non-independent, and the rear axle was bolted direct to the chassis. The engine was a supercharged Chrysler V8, running on methanol and developing around 400 bhp. In a standing ¼-mile, Allard did 10·48 seconds in one of the first acceleration demonstrations in Britain. Sydney Allard was one of the prime movers in getting Drag Racing organized in Britain, but by the time of the first Drag Festivals in the mid-60s he had retired from active competition. He died in 1966 at the early age of 56.

Sydney Allard driving his Steyr-powered Special at the Bo'ness hill-climb in Scotland in 1949, the year he won the RAC Hill-climb Championship

Year: 1949
Model: Sprint
Engine: Steyr (air-cooled)
Number of cylinders: 8 in-vee
Bore and Stroke: 79 × 92 mm
Capacity: 3600 cc
Valves: Inclined overhead with pushrods
Induction: Eight Amal carburettors
Wheelbase: 8 ft 4 in
Forward Speeds: 3
Front Suspension: Independent by transverse leaf spring and swing axles
Rear Suspension: de Dion with coil springs
Chassis Frame: Channel-section
Maximum Speed: 140 mph

Alta

Though small in size the Alta Car & Engineering Company of Tolworth, Surrey, was not small in ideas and efforts. Starting with sports cars in the early '30s, Geoffrey Taylor, the man behind the Alta, soon produced 1½- and 2-litre racing cars suitable for British races, sprints and hill-climbs. The first cars were narrower versions of the sports cars, with the 4-cylinder 2-ohc supercharged engine set to the left of the channel-section chassis frame, with the ENV preselector gearbox and rear axle final drive unit also set to the left. This allowed the driver to sit low, alongside the propellor-shaft, and yet kept the overall width fairly narrow.

right Geoffrey Taylor in the cockpit of the Abecassis Alta in the Brooklands paddock in 1937

below George Abecassis in the post-war GP Alta in 1950

The Alta was one of the earliest British racing cars to dispense with the conventional and distinctive radiator shell, Taylor using a radiator block behind a curved-nose cowling. In 1937 he built a very narrow single-seater racing car, with independent suspension to all four wheels by means of coil springs and vertical slides. At the rear were two springs to each wheel with the drive-shaft passing between them. While Alta engines gave plenty of power they were designed and built down to a price, and in consequence safety limits were a bit low and they were none too reliable over long periods. However, this supercharged 1½-litre 4-cylinder car was raced successfully in short races by George Abecassis, frequently chasing the all-conquering ERAs in British events and occasionally beating them. Three of these advanced single-seaters were built, and the last one, raced by Tony Beadle, had a tubular chassis frame and reduction gear rear axle and was a lot lower; it had a 2-litre engine.

Taylor was always imaginative and he could supply his engines with alternative wet liners to give $1\frac{1}{2}$- or 2-litres capacity. In 1939 he built another single-seater with torsion bar suspension, still independent all round, which was very advanced for a 'voiturette' in pre-war days, but the outbreak of war prevented this car from being raced. In November 1945 he was back in motor racing, offering for sale an entirely new car, using the same basic engine design, but now of square bore and stroke, 78×78 mm, as against the pre-war $1\frac{1}{2}$-litre's 69×100 mm. An ENV gearbox was retained, but the design had a new tubular chassis and independent suspension to all wheels by means of wishbones and rubber blocks in compression. In the immediate post-war years Taylor progressed with supercharged $1\frac{1}{2}$-litre cars for the then current GP Formula, eventually building a 2-stage supercharged version of his 4-cylinder engine. He built unsupercharged 2-litre 4-cylinder engines for the HWM team and in 1952–3 he built new Formula 2 Altas, with his own manufactured syncromesh gearbox. In those days the Alta engine was the only real racing engine on sale in Great Britain and, apart from HWM, other private owners used them.

In 1954 when Connaught tackled Formula 1 GP racing seriously they contracted for Taylor to build them $2\frac{1}{2}$-litre 4-cylinder engines, which they developed extensively until it gave 250 bhp. With the demise of Connaught Racing there was no further call for Alta engines and Geoffrey Taylor retired from business and wound up the Alta Car & Engineering Company. He died at the comparatively early age of 63 in 1966, but his young son Michael was developing a keen interest in motor racing and in 1976 he achieved a personal ambition in the reforming of the Alta Car & Engineering Company, in association with Mike Barney a former Cooper and Brabham mechanic. The new company was formed in a small works in Epsom, not far from Tolworth, where his father's firm had been. Mike Taylor's first car-building effort was directed at a Formula Ford single-seater, using a Rowland-tuned Ford Cortina-based engine and a Hewland gearbox and transmission. The new car is known as the Alta BT1F.

Year: 1937
Model: 'Voiturette'
Engine: Alta
Number of cylinders: 4
Bore and Stroke: 68.75×100
Capacity: 1488 cc
Valves: Inclined overhead with twin ohcs

Induction: Supercharged
Wheelbase: 8 ft 0 in
Forward Speeds: 4 ENV preselector
Front and Rear Suspension:
Independent by vertical coil springs and sliding pillars
Chassis Frame: Channel-section
Maximum Speed: 130 mph

Year: 1950
Model: F1 GP
Engine: Alta
Number of cylinders: 4
Bore and Stroke: 78 × 78 mm
Capacity: 1490 cc
Valves: Inclined overhead with two ohcs

Induction: Two-stage supercharging
Wheelbase: 8 ft 5 in
Forward Speeds: 4 ENV preselector
Front and Rear Suspension:
Independent by wishbones and
rubber blocks in compression
Chassis Frame: Tubular
Maximum Speed: 150 mph

Amon-Dalton
England

After some frustrating times with various Formula 1 teams, New Zealander Chris Amon thought there could not be that much difficulty in building a Formula 1 car, using all the accepted proprietary items like Cosworth DFV engine, Hewland transmission, Girling brakes, Armstrong shock-absorbers etc. In a fit of enthusiasm Amon's friend John Dalton agreed to finance the idea and they contacted a young designer, Gordon Fowell, who had been doing general design work and had met Amon when he designed a chassis for the ill-fated Tecno car. He had also been working on sports-car projects.

Chris Amon in the unfortunate Amon-Dalton Formula 1 car during the Spanish GP at the Jarama Autodrome in 1974

The Amon-Dalton, as the car was called, made its debut at the 1974 Spanish GP but obviously had a long way to go to become competitive. It had many good ideas and many detail differences from accepted practice, such as torsion bar springing, titanium suspension parts, inboard front brakes and a forward seating position with the fuel tanks between the driver and the engine, and not on each side of the cockpit. It was quite an advanced design, but the team was too small to do the job properly. John Dalton found that building the car was only half the financial battle, developing the finished car and maintaining a team was another matter altogether. By mid-season both he and Amon realized they would be better off to cut their losses. The final blow came when the car was crashed in practice at the Nurburgring by Larry Perkins, who was substituting for an unwell Amon.

As an example of misguided enthusiasm the Amon-Dalton is not alone, there were many before it and no doubt there are more to come.

Year: 1974
Model: AF101
Engine: Cosworth DFV
Number of cylinders: 8 in-vee
Bore and Stroke: 85·6 × 64·8 mm
Capacity: 2993 cc
Valves: 4 per cylinder, two ohcs per bank
Induction: Lucas fuel-injection
Wheelbase: 8 ft 4in
Forward Speeds: 5 Hewland

Front Suspension: Independent by unequal length wishbones and torsion bars
Rear Suspension: Independent by upper wishbone, lower parallel links, radius rods and torsion bar
Chassis Frame: Aluminium monocoque; engine a stressed member
Maximum Speed: 170 mph

Appleton Special   England

In 1934 R.J.W. Appleton bought a 1100-cc Maserati, with a rather under-powered engine, and replaced it with a tuned 4-cylinder Riley Nine engine. He shortened the chassis, fitted a preselector gearbox from an MG and a large Zoller supercharger which blew at 25 lb/in^2, and the engine developed 118 bhp. This naturally inspired him to greater developments and his next move was to reduce the width of the chassis to make it a very narrow single-seater, at the same time developing the engine still further. A new body was built which was similar to the then all-conquering Mercedes-Benz GP cars, with a cowled radiator and a large head fairing on the pointed tail.

By 1936 the engine development had reached such a state that practically all the moving parts had been redesigned and specially made, including a massive three-bearing crankshaft which was made to fit into the standard Riley cylinder-block casting. In short races at Brooklands and Donington Park, and in hill-climbs and sprints, Appleton had a great deal of success and in 1937 he set up International Class G records over the standing-start kilometre and mile, the figures being 82·1 mph and 91·3 mph.

For the 1938 season the Appleton Special, as it was now called, underwent some major changes, having a large Arnott supercharger fitted in place of the Zoller, blowing at 27 lb/in^2 and some special camshafts, and over 160 bhp was developed. This work was done by Robin Jackson and 'Sinbad' Milledge at Jackson's tuning establishment at Brooklands track. A new and slimmer body was built and the maximum speed was now around 130 mph while the weight was down to 12¾ cwt. The car was known everywhere for its ear-splitting exhaust note, which put the contemporary ERA in the shade! Attention to the valve gear raised the rpm and the power output, until a maximum test-bed reading of 183 bhp was recorded. By now the engine was a bit temperamental and had a distressing habit of bursting rather violently. The writer well recalls one of these occasions, at a speed trial, when the high-pitched crackle of the exhaust suddenly lost its edge and the head of an exhaust valve, together with bits of stem came out of the exhaust pipe!

The war put a stop to the development of the Appleton Special, and though it appeared in the post-war era when John Appleton sold it, without the backing of the Jackson tuning shop it never performed quite as before. Over the years it passed through many hands, and at one point the special 1100-cc engine was removed and a fairly normal unblown 1½-litre Riley engine was installed. In subsequent changes of ownership the special Riley engine was 'lost' and the present owners have supercharged the 1½-litre engine and turned the Appleton Special into a very successful car for VSCC racing.

Year: 1934/39
Model: Special
Engine: Riley
Number of cylinders: 4
Bore and Stroke: 60·3 × 95·2 mm
Capacity: 1089 cc
Valves: Inclined overhead with pushrods
Induction: Supercharged
Wheelbase: 7 ft 6 in
Forward Speeds: 4 ENV preselector
Front and Rear Suspension: Semi-elliptic leaf springs
Chassis Frame: Channel-section
Maximum Speed: 135 mph
NB—Now fitted with 4-cylinder 69 × 100-mm Riley 1½-litre engine

The Appleton Special in its ultimate pre-war guise with inter-cooler protruding from the bonnet and complex three-pane windscreen

Arzani-Volpini Italy

The two Milanese enthusiasts Egidio Arzani and Gianpaolo Volpini acquired the last-built supercharged 1½-litre Milan car of 1950 from the Ruggeri brothers and in 1954 rebuilt it to use in the new Formula for 2½-litre cars. The engine was enlarged to 2496 cc by making a new crankshaft and increasing the bore diameter, while the two-stage supercharging was replaced by Weber carburettors and the car renamed the Arzani-Volpini. It was not a great success, appearing but twice in 1955, the first time in the Pau Grand Prix and the second time in practice for the Italian Grand Prix. After that it was not seen again.

The Arzani-Volpini seen in 1955 before going to the Pau GP

Year: 1954
Model: F1
Engine: Maserati-Milan
Number of cylinders: 4
Bore and Stroke: 94 × 90 mm
Capacity: 2496 cc
Valves: Inclined overhead with twin ohcs
Induction: Two double-choke Weber carburettors

Wheelbase: 8 ft 2¾ in.
Forward Speeds: 4
Front Suspension: Independent by double wishbones and torsion bars
Rear Suspension: Independent by trailing arms and transverse leaf spring
Chassis Frame: Oval tubes
Maximum Speed: 140 mph

Aston Martin   England

Lionel Martin began by building sporting cars with side-valve engines which he used in hill-climbs, the Aston part of the name being derived from the Aston Clinton hill-climb where he was a regular competitor. In 1921, in partnership with Robert Bamford, he was producing sports cars, still with quite fast 1½-litre side-valve engines, and in 1922, financed by Count Zborowski, the firm built some 1½-litre, 16-valve, 4-cylinder, twin-ohc cars, for 'voiturette' and GP racing, the design inspired by the famous Ernest Henry, who at that time was passing from Ballot to Sunbeam.

These little GP-type cars ran very successfully, supplementing the racing achievements of special side-valve cars at Brooklands and at hill-climbs, and in the 1½-litre class the name Aston Martin became famous. Zborowski's death in 1924 put paid to the future of the racing 16-valve, twin-cam cars and also to the firm, as he had been financing it. The name was revived in 1926 with new backers, but racing interests lay only with sports cars with which they were highly successful.

The Aston Martin company passed through other hands, and it was not until 1959 that another GP Aston Martin appeared on the racing circuits. By this time David Brown was the owner and had established the name as a most worthy large sports and GT car, the competition sports Aston Martins in the DB range having had a long and successful career. It was intended to build GP cars for the 1954 Formula of 2½-lites, but sports-car racing and production work delayed the project, so that when they did appear they were too late. Design trends had changed drastically and the DBR4/250 with its 6-cylinder twin-ohc engine at the front, in a heavy chassis, with de Dion rear end, was outdated. The era of the small rear-engine racing car was well under way, and though raced during 1959 and 1960 the Aston Martins were never successful.

Had the Aston Martin appeared in 1954 or 1955 it could well have proved a very successful GP car, but as it was it just faded quietly away when David Brown withdrew from all forms of competition in 1961. It does have the doubtful distinction of being one of the last, if not the last, GP car to use a de Dion axle layout, the era of the small rear-engined cars encouraging the design of i.r.s. and even Aston Martin used this on their last GP car in 1960. Four models of the DBR4 were built in 1959 and two subsequent DBR5 models in 1960. Of the first series three remain, one in the Donington Racing Car museum and two in the hands of VSCC members. These three cars went to Australia in 1960 and were used with 3-litre Aston Martin engines installed. The car raced in Historic events by Neil Corner is still in this form. The two 1960 cars were scrapped by the factory when they withdrew from racing.

The DBR4/250 Aston Martin single-seater photographed on its completion in 1959, still lacking a few details like mirrors and seat

Year: 1922
Model: Grand Prix
Engine: Aston Martin
Number of cylinders: 4
Bore and Stroke: 65 × 112 mm
Capacity: 1487 cc
Valves: Inclined overhead with
two ohcs

Induction: Two carburettors
Wheelbase: 7 ft 6 in
Forward Speeds: 4
Front and Rear Suspension:
Semi-elliptic leaf springs
Chassis Frame: Channel-section
Maximum Speed: 105 mph

Year: 1959
Model: F1 DBR4/250
Engine: Aston Martin
Number of cylinders: 6
Bore and Stroke: 83 × 76·8 mm
Capacity: 2492 cc
Valves: Inclined overhead with
two ohcs

Wheelbase: 7 ft 6 in
Forward Speeds: 5
Front Suspension: Independent by
double wishbones and coil springs
Rear Suspension: de Dion with
torsion bars
Chassis Frame: Tubular space-frame
Maximum Speed: 160 mph

ATS

Italy

At the end of 1961 a number of top personnel in the Scuderia Ferrari walked out with the avowed intent of setting up a rival concern to beat Enzo Ferrari at his own game. They were led by designer Carlo Chiti and team manager Romolo Tavoni, and had the backing of the rich Count Giovanni Volpi, together with businessman Jaime Ortiz Patiño and industrialist Giorgio Billi. In a very short time they had set up a new factory at Sasso Marconi, just south of Bologna and the company was known as Automobili Turismo e Sport (ATS). Drivers Phil Hill and Giancarlo Baghetti had also been lured away from Ferrari, and by the end of 1962 the first Formula 1 car had been completed.

Phil Hill in the Tipo 100 ATS during the 1963 Belgian GP on the Francorchamps circuit

Not unnaturally the general layout was very Ferrari-like, but the engine was a 90-degree V8 with four ohcs and the 6-speed gearbox was between the engine and the rear axle. Count Volpi had left the concern early on, to start his own Scuderia Serenissima, and at no time did there seem to be complete harmony among those involved with the firm. As well as the Formula 1 car a mid-engined GT coupé was produced, and the whole project seemed to be too ambitious for the size of the firm.

The Formula 1 cars made their appearance in 1963, and Hill and Baghetti drove them in the Belgian GP, but they were quite hopeless. Other races were contested with little in the way of success or even hope, and after a fruitless trip to America for the races at Watkins Glen and Mexico City, the whole team collapsed. The factory carried on for a while doing sub-contract engineering work, but the ATS as a challenge to Ferrari was dead.

Today Carlo Chiti is the chief engine designer for the Auto Delta competition branch of Alfa Romeo, and Romolo Tavoni is on the executive of the Monza Autodromo.

Year: 1963
Model: Tipo 100—Formula 1
Engine: ATS
Number of cylinders: 8 in-vee
Bore and Stroke: 66 × 54·6 mm
Capacity: 1494 cc
Valves: Inclined overhead with two ohcs per bank
Induction: Lucas fuel-injection
Wheelbase: 7 ft 7⅜ in (2320 mm)

Forward Speeds: 6-speed ATS-Colotti
Front Suspension: Independent by wishbone and rocker arm with inboard coil spring/damper unit
Rear Suspension: Independent by wishbones, links and coil springs
Chassis Frame: Tubular space-frame
Maximum Speed: 145 mph

Austin   England

After competing in the 1908 GP the Austin Motor Company did not feature strongly in motor racing until shortly after the advent of the remarkable Austin 7. The sports Brooklands models, and later Ulster models of the ubiquitous 'baby' Austin, were soon used as the basis for single-seater racing cars, both unblown and blown.

A stripped side-valve Ulster 2-seater won the 1930 BRDC 500 Mile Race at the very respectable speed of 83·41 mph, and the following year the factory produced a team of tiny single-seaters, using Ulster parts, with short pointed tails which, due to their shape, were dubbed the 'Dutch Clogs'. These were followed by improved versions of pure racing Austin 7 models, highly supercharged, and by 1934 the works blown side-valve Austin 7 was remarkably fast and able to give a good account of itself, notably driven by Pat Driscoll.

As the power was increased the engine became less and less standard, as did the chassis and suspension, but the basic layout of the Austin 7 was always followed. T. Murray Jamieson had joined the racing department by this time and was responsible for engine development and the ultimate in works side-valve engines had special blocks with 32 studs holding down the alloy head, for supercharger pressures were very high. It also featured two sparking plugs per cylinder and ran on very special alcohol fuel. Parallel with this racing programme Sir Herbert Austin carried out a factory programme of record breaking, over short distances, with very streamlined versions of his road-racing cars.

The 'twin-cam' Austin, driven by H.L. Hadley, seen by the pits at Donington Park in 1939. The cockpit-side bulge gives space for the gear-lever

In 1936 an entirely new works car was designed by Murray Jamieson, and this was really a miniature GP car, scaled down to 750 cc as Sir Herbert insisted that his racing cars should appear to be Austin 7s. This new car was the twin-overhead camshaft, supercharged 744-cc Austin, with its remarkable little engine capable of 9000 rpm and good for over 125 mph. The Austin 7 principles of layout were still followed, front suspension being non-independent by transverse leaf-spring, and the rigid rear axle mounted on splayed quarter-elliptic springs. The engine was quite small, completely dominated by the twin-overhead camshaft cylinder head, and the supercharger was behind the engine, above the 4-speed gearbox. Wheels of 16-in diameter kept the proportions of this little racer extremely neat, and the single-seater body with its radiator cowl and head fairing behind the driver made it look like a small Mercedes-Benz GP car, especially as they appeared in their first season painted white.

These twin-cam Austins were raced up to the war in 1939, the drivers being Pat Driscoll, Charles Goodacre, Charlie Dodson and Bert Hadley, the last driver carrying the Austin fortunes to the last race before war put a stop to everything. A team of three twin-cam cars was built, one being destroyed by an accident and the other two being supplemented by one of the side-valve cars, usually driven by Mrs. Kay Petre. The works team raced only in the British Isles, although one car was lent to a German driver on occasions to run at the Nurburgring and in hill-climbs. They were particularly successful at Donington Park and the Crystal Palace, and Hadley won the last race of 1939 at the latter circuit.

The racing team was never restarted after the war and though the Austin company retained the cars they were sadly neglected. When the Austin Motor Company was absorbed into the British Motor Corporation all hope of ever seeing a works racing Austin again in competition was gone. However, with the advent of Tom Wheatcroft's Racing Car Museum at Donington Park, one of the twin-cam cars and the remaining side-valve car were loaned to him and he had them both stripped completely and rebuilt to full working order. They now reside at Donington in perfect condition and are often given an airing, the writer having driven both of them at racing speeds and found them to be really delightful little 'babies'. The twin-cam car is the one raced by Charlie Dodson, while the side-valve car is the sprint and hill-climb model. The long-distance racing version of the side-valve car was destroyed in a crash at Brooklands in 1937. Recently, the engine and gearbox from this car was built into a facsimile of the original car and can be seen in VSCC events. The twin-cam car driven by Hadley is on display in the National Motor Museum at Beaulieu but has not been rebuilt.

Year: 1936
Model: Twin-cam
Engine: Austin
Number of cylinders: 4
Bore and Stroke: 60·3 × 65·1 mm
Capacity: 744 cc
Valves: Inclined overhead with two ohcs
Induction: Roots supercharger

Wheelbase: 6 ft 10 in
Forward Speeds: 4
Front Suspension: Transverse leaf spring
Rear Suspension: Splayed quarter-elliptic leaf springs
Chassis Frame: Channel-section
Maximum Speed: 125 mph

Auto Union   Germany

With the beginning of a new racing Formula in 1934 a fresh name appeared in GP racing—Auto Union—and it was a racing organization supported by four German motor manufacturers, Audi, Wanderer, Horch and DKW; the badge of the Auto Union comprized four interlocking rings, representing the four parent companies. In 1933 Dr. Ferdinand Porsche had completed the designs for a remarkable 16-cylinder supercharged rear-engined racing car, with independent suspension to all four wheels, and he sold this design to the newly formed Auto Union and joined them as consultant designer and development engineer.

The Auto Union engine was noted for its enormous power of well over 500 bhp and the fact that it was able to use an engine of over 6-litres capacity and still not exceed the maximum formula limit of 750 kilogrammes. It was not an easy car to handle, but such drivers as Stuck, Varzi and Rosemeyer became particularly adept at racing these fierce rear-engined cars, and the battles they waged with the powerful Mercedes-Benz team in the years 1934–39 have become legendary. In the early Auto Unions the driver sat very far foward, the long tapering tail containing the engine and 5-speed gearbox, seemingly stretching out to eternity behind him. Due to this layout the cars were prone to sliding their rear wheels out on corners, and full-opposite-lock cornering was the typical stance for an Auto Union in a hurry.

A 1936 C-type Auto Union with spinning rear wheels driven by Hans Stuck at the Nurburgring in the German GP

The rear-mounted engine meant plenty of weight over the rear wheels and good adhesion for acceleration, and Dr. Porsche got his drivers to demonstrate this by setting up world record figures for a standing-start mile and kilometre that stood until very recently, the mile record being improved upon only in 1960. Their maximum speed was equally impressive and in streamlined form with the 6-litre engine, one of these cars set records at 199 mph in 1935. Later in this pre-war period of German supremacy a special record-breaking Auto Union, developed from the GP car but with all-enveloping bodywork, achieved nearly 270 mph on a German Autobahn.

With the change in the GP rules for 1938 and 1939, Auto Union built 12-cylinder 3-litre cars, with de Dion rear suspension and longer noses, the driver being seated further back than in the original designs. Dr. Porsche left the combine and his place was taken by Prof. Dr. Ing. Eberan von Eberhorst. Nuvolari was their star driver and with these cars he won the last GP to be held at Donington Park in 1938, and also the last GP to run prior to the Second World War—in Belgrade on the day war was declared. With the Auto Union factory being in the East Zone of Germany the racing department was never resurrected after the war, and the cars had been destroyed during hostilities, except for one very early chassis that had been prepared for the 1934 Berlin Motor Show and had then been transferred to the Deutsches Museum in Munich, where it is still on display. Recently one of the 12-cylinder 3-litre cars of 1939 was discovered in Czechoslovakia and made a brief appearance at a gathering in France in 1974, but it was not in running order. However, it was the first time one of these remarkable cars had been seen for 35 years.

To anyone who never saw these unusual racing cars in action they might seem to be legends, but equally, anyone who heard the 16-cylinder engines in action will never forget them.

Year: 1936
Model: C-type
Engine: Auto Union
Number of cylinders: 16 in-vee
Bore and Stroke: 75 × 85 mm
Capacity: 6010 cc
Valves: Inclined overhead with one ohc and horizontal pushrods
Induction: Roots supercharger
Wheelbase: 9 ft 6½ in

Forward Speeds: 4
Front Suspension: Independent by trailing arms and transverse torsion bars
Rear Suspension: Independent by swing axles and longitudinal torsion bars
Chassis Frame: Tubular ladder-type
Maximum Speed: 195 mph

Year: 1939
Model: D-type
Engine: Auto Union
Number of cylinders: 12 in-vee
Bore and Stroke: 65 × 75 mm
Capacity: 2988 cc
Valves: Inclined overhead with three ohcs
Induction: Two-stage Roots superchargers

Wheelbase: 9 ft 4 in
Forward Speeds: 5
Front Suspension: Independent by trailing arms and transverse torsion bars
Rear Suspension: de Dion with longitudinal torsion bars
Chassis Frame: Tubular ladder-type
Maximum Speed: 185 mph

Barnato-Hassan   England

In 1934 Captain Woolf Barnato decided to sponsor a Brooklands track-racing car and he used his sports 6½-litre Bentley for the job. Walter Hassan, who had been with the Bentley racing team, and later was to join Jaguar and Coventry-

Climax, was responsible for the work. He converted the 4-seater car into an offset single-seater. It had underslung rear springs, with the chassis frame passing under the axle, a cowled radiator and pointed tail with head fairing. On its first outing, in the 1934 BRDC 500 Mile Race, it lapped at 115 mph, but the engine protested and burst.

Hassan acquired a new 8-litre 6-cylinder Bentley engine and installed it in the Barnato-Hassan. The engine was tuned and modified, having new connecting rods and pistons, the compression ratio raised to 7·5:1, and later to 8·7:1, while alcohol fuel was used for the three SU carburettors. In 1935 Oliver Bertram drove the car and took the Class B lap record at 137·73 mph and later the all-comers' lap record at 142·60 mph. In 1936 the car was modified still further, the chassis was narrowed aft of the engine, the steering placed in the centre, and a very narrow body fitted that was so tightly wrapped round the engine that the tops of the carburettors and one magneto protruded through holes. The three SU carburettors were fed by a long, forward-facing air intake that extended beyond the radiator cowl and was said to show $\frac{1}{2}$ lb/in^2 supercharge at 140 mph! The front brakes were dispensed with as the car was only used for track-racing, and the colour was changed from green to silver-blue.

In this form the car raced in Outer Circuit events up to the end of 1938, driven by Oliver Bertram, but finally was withdrawn as it was having an impossible task to beat the handicappers, even though it was lapping at 142 mph. Although it never retook the lap record from Cobb's Napier-Railton, it was often very close to it and on one of its last appearances lapped at 143·11 mph, to be the second fastest car ever to run on the Brooklands track.

After the war it was sold and the new owner converted it into a 2-seater sports car, with bulbous body that caused it to be dubbed 'The Whale', though it was officially just a Bentley 8-litre. It ran in one or two immediate post-war sports-car races, and then was used in British club racing at Silverstone. Finally Keith Schellenberg acquired it and converted it back to a

left The Barnato-Hassan in 1938 in the Brooklands paddock with Oliver Bertram in the cockpit and Woolf Barnato and Wally Hassan alongside

right Reg Parnell in the BHW Special at the Syston Park speed trials in 1939

single-seater of something like its original shape, and it is frequently seen in VSCC events today.

After building the Barnato-Hassan, Wally built a similar car around 4½-litre Bentley parts for E.W.W. Pacey, and the Pacey-Hassan was a regular Brooklands competitor. Though not as fast as the Barnato, it was very successful, frequently beating its handicap, and it finished 2nd in the 1936 BRDC 500 Mile Race. It also appears in VSCC events today.

Year: 1934/36
Model: Special
Engine: Bentley
Number of cylinders: 6
Bore and Stroke: 110 × 140 mm
Capacity: 7963 cc
Valves: Overhead with single ohc
Induction: Three SU carburettors

Wheelbase: 11 ft 6 in
Forward Speeds: 4
Front Suspension: Semi-elliptic leaf springs
Rear Suspension: Underslung semi-elliptic leaf springs
Chassis Frame: Channel-section
Maximum Speed: 160 mph

BHW   Anglo-French

Building specials has always been popular with British racing enthusiasts and just before the last war a very powerful racing car was concocted for use in national events. This was the BHW special, which was commissioned by Dick Wilkins, and designed by Wally Hassan, and as the engine was a Bugatti, the initials BHW were adopted. The engine was a straight-8 supercharged of 4·9 litres, which was taken from the famous Type 54 Bugatti raced at Brooklands by Kaye Don. Walter Hassan built a new chassis frame, with independent front suspension and a new rear suspension using splayed-out quarter-elliptic springs.

This project was completed in 1938, and raced by A.P. Hamilton and the

owner. The following year it was bought by Reg Parnell, who ran it at Brooklands, Donington Park and in hill-climbs. As the engine dated back to 1931 it was beginning to get rather temperamental and unreliable. After the war it passed through numerous hands but was never made to go properly, and it finally ended up in a private motor collection in Scotland. Eventually it was broken up and the Bugatti engine was sold. The original Type 54 Bugatti from which the engine was taken was fitted for a short time with the Vauxhall Villiers supercharged engine, but when that power unit was returned to its original chassis the Type 54, complete less engine and gearbox, was put on one side and still lies in a private collection.

Year: 1938
Model: Special
Engine: Bugatti
Number of cylinders: 8 in-line
Bore and Stroke: 86 × 107 mm
Capacity: 4975 cc
Valves: Inclined overhead with two ohcs
Induction: Supercharged

Wheelbase: 9 ft 0 in
Forward Speeds: 3
Front Suspension: Independent by transverse leaf spring and wishbones
Rear Suspension: Independent by swing axles and quarter-elliptic leaf springs
Chassis Frame: Channel-section
Maximum Speed: 150 mph

BMW   Germany

The name of the Bayerische Motoren Werke (BMW) has been connected with sports-car racing for a long time, but it was not until 1966 that a single-seater racing car first appeared from the Munich factory. This was a 2-litre 4-cylinder hill-climb car, using a racing BMW engine in a Brabham chassis. The engine used a special cylinder head designed by Ludwig Apfelbeck in which four valves per cylinder were arranged radially and operated by rockers from two overhead camshafts. The following year a 1·6-litre version of this was built for the new Formula 2 and mounted in a Lola chassis, but after one season they had their own chassis designed and built by the Dornier company in full monocoque form.

A new cylinder-head layout was used, of more conventional 4-valve layout, and the factory ran a team of three cars with two types of bodywork, one being more streamlined than the other, for use on fast circuits. The 1·6-litre engine was giving 225 bhp at 10,300 rpm and during 1970 the cars were quite successful in Formula 2. At the end of the season the BMW withdrew from single-seater racing and turned to saloon-car racing, as it had a more direct application to production cars. The 4-cylinder BMW engine in various sizes was made available to chassis constructors for both single-seater and sports-car competition and the Formula 2 version completely dominated that category.

Hubert Hahne in the factory BMW with 2-litre Apfelbeck engine in a Lola chassis during the 1968 German GP

Year: 1969
Model: Formula 2
Engine: BMW-M20
Number of cylinders: 4
Bore and Stroke: 89 × 64 mm
Capacity: 1596 cc
Valves: 4 per cylinder with two ohcs
Induction: Fuel-injection
Wheelbase: 6 ft 10¼ in

Forward Speeds: 5-Hewland
Front Suspension: Double wishbones and coil springs
Rear Suspension: Transverse links, radius rods and coil springs
Chassis Frame: Aluminium monocoque with tubular engine bay (Lola T102)
Maximum Speed: 160 mph

Bolster Special   England

The name of John Bolster ranks as a classic in the special builders field. As an undergraduate he built his first racing special for sprints and hill-climbs, using a V-twin JAP engine, the comparative success of which encouraged him to become more ambitious. He acquired a second V-twin JAP engine of 980 cc and fitted both engines into his light wooden chassis. By the time the two engines were installed and coupled together by driving chains, as well as the gearbox and final drive, there was little enough room for Bolster, and he literally sat alongside the chains, with his right elbow almost touching a rear wheel. The whole mechanism amply justified the term 'contraption', and Bolster called in 'Bloody Mary'. Having engines totalling 2-litres capacity and very light overall weight, this car was a force to be reckoned with in hill-climbs and sprints in the '30s.

In 1938 he built a new special, this time with a modern steel box-section chassis and independent front suspension, as well as powerful brakes and steering more in keeping with the speed of the car. Into this chassis he squeezed four V-twin JAP engines, giving a total capacity of almost 4 litres, mounted in pairs side-by-side. They were all coupled to a single clutch by chains, and then via the usual motor-cycle gearbox and chains to the rear axle. Once Bolster had got all four engines firing in unison the power of this tiny vehicle was phenomenal and he took part in short races at Brooklands and the Crystal Palace, but all that mechanism was really too much for one man, and the car never achieved the success of 'Bloody Mary'.

After the war Bolster abandoned the 4-engined car and put two of the engines back into 'Mary', and she returned to the racing scene in all her old glory. The immediate post-war hill-climbing scene was much enlivened by Bolster and 'Bloody Mary' until he retired from competitions. However, they are both still in the motoring world for John Bolster is Technical Editor of *Autosport*, and 'Mary' lies quietly in the National Motor Museum at Beaulieu. Whether he ever actually managed to control her is still open to doubt, for a climb of Prescott by the two of them resembled little more than an unruly brawl between man and machine, but the resultant time was usually among the fastest.

John Bolster leaving the Esses at Shelsley Walsh in 1938 in his 4-engined 4-litre special

Year: 1934
Model: Bloody Mary
Engines: JAP
Number of cylinders: 4, two vee-twins
Bore and Stroke: 85·7 × 85 mm
Capacity: 1962 cc
Valves: Overhead with pushrods
Induction: Carburettors
Wheelbase: 6 ft 8 in
Forward Speeds: 4
Front and Rear Suspension: Quarter-elliptic leaf springs
Chassis Frame: Wood
Maximum Speed: 100 mph

Brabham   Australian

Driving for the Cooper works team, Australian Jack Brabham not only won the Drivers' World Championship in 1959 and 1960, but had become mainly responsible for the design work on the cars. It was no surprise when he left the Cooper Car Company and set up in business on his own to build racing cars for sale. A long-time friend from Australia joined him to do the design work, and the influence of Ron Tauranac can be seen throughout the racing world even to this day.

In 1961 they completed their first car, a Ford-powered Formula Junior car, which they called MRD, these being the initials of their firm, Motor

Racing Developments Ltd. Unfortunately the initials MRD are pronounced 'merde' in French, and with Brabham hoping to sell cars in Europe he was advised to change the name! This Formula Junior car went into production as a Brabham, and more than 30 were sold; meanwhile Jack was at work on a new Formula 1 car for himself, powered by a V8 Coventry-Climax engine and the BT3 appeared towards the end of 1962.

The firm flourished with sales of small racing cars, powered by proprietary engines, while Brabham himself continued to race in Formula 1, using the Coventry-Climax engine until the end of the 1½-litre Formula in 1965. He ran a two-car team from the works, while Ron Tauranac concentrated on the building and selling of small Formula cars. When the new 3-litre Formula 1 was introduced in 1966, Jack Brabham had not wasted any time and appeared with a new car powered by a V8 Repco engine, designed by Phil Irving, using an Oldsmobile V8 as the basis. The Brabham-Repco V8 was a comparatively

Jack Brabham in a Cosworth-powered BT33 winning the South African GP in 1970, his last racing season before retiring

simple car, but very functional, won not only the Drivers' Championship for 1966, but also the Manufacturers' Championship, the first time an 'owner-driver' had accomplished this. The following year was another Brabham-Repco year, this time Denny Hulme winning the championship. Meanwhile, Jack Brabham had come to an arrangement with the Honda Motor Company of Japan, to run their new Formula 2 engines in his works cars for himself and Hulme, and between them they were unbeatable in this category. All this time the Formula 3 cars were selling well and were known as Repco-Brabhams, in acknowledgement of the firms Formula 1 sponsor. A 4-cam Repco V8 was built in the Australian works for the 1968 Formula 1 season, but this engine was not so successful, and for 1969 Jack Brabham went the Cosworth DFV route and abandoned the Repco engines. Brabham cars with Cosworth power carried him through to his retirement at the end of 1970 and were still the motive power in the Tauranac cars when the firm was sold to Bernard Ecclestone.

After selling the firm Jack Brabham returned to his native Australia, while Tauranac left and started up a firm of his own. The new owner of Motor Racing Developments has kept the name Brabham, even though there is no longer any direct connection, the new BT45 cars, with Alfa Romeo engines, being the entire work of Gordon Murray. Throughout the life of the real Brabham firm there had always been cars for sale, especially for Formula 3 and similar categories, but under the new management this activity ceased and now the only Brabham cars are those operated by the works team.

Year: 1962
Model: BT3—Formula 1
Engine: Coventry Climax
Number of cylinders: 8 in-vee
Bore and Stroke: 63 × 60 mm
Capacity: 1494 cc
Valves: Inclined overhead with four ohcs
Induction: Lucas fuel-injection

Wheelbase: 7 ft 7 in
Forward Speeds: 5
Front Suspension: Double wishbones and coil springs
Rear Suspension: Wishbone, link, radius rods and coil springs
Chassis Frame: Tubular space-frame
Maximum Speed: 160 mph

Year: 1966
Model: BT 16—Formula 2
Engine: Honda
Number of cylinders: 4
Bore and Stroke: 78 × 52 mm
Capacity: 996 cc
Valves: Four per cylinder with two ohcs
Induction: Fuel injection

Wheelbase: 7 ft 7¾ in
Forward Speeds: 6
Front Suspension: Double wishbones and coil springs
Rear Suspension: Wishbone, link, radius rods and coil springs
Chassis Frame: Tubular space-frame
Maximum Speed: 145 mph

Year: 1969
Model: BT26A—Formula 1
Engine: Cosworth DFV
Number of cylinders: 8 in-vee
Bore and Stroke: 85·6 × 64·8 mm
Capacity: 2993 cc
Valves: 4 per cylinder, two ohcs per bank
Induction: Lucas fuel-injection

Wheelbase: 7 ft 11 in
Forward Speeds: 5
Front Suspension: Double wishbones and coil springs
Rear Suspension: Wishbone, link, radius rods and coil springs
Chassis Frame: Tubular space-frame
Maximum Speed: 175–180 mph

Year: 1977
Model: BT45B—Formula 1
Engine: Alfa Romeo
Number of cylinders: 12 horizontally-opposed
Bore and Stroke: 77 × 53·6 mm
Capacity: 2995 cc
Valves: 4 per cylinder, two ohcs per bank
Induction: Fuel-injection

Wheelbase: 8 ft 2 in
Forward Speeds: 6
Front Suspension: Wishbones and coil springs
Rear Suspension: Transverse links, radius rods and coil springs
Chassis Frame: Aluminium monocoque
Maximum Speed: 185 mph

BRM   England

The BRM started as the brainchild of Raymond Mays, who, together with Peter Berthon, schemed out the idea of a racing car built and financed by members of the British motor industry and accessory manufacturers. A team of mechanics and technicians were to assemble and race the cars from the

top Froilan Gonzalez driving a BRM 16-cylinder at Goodwood in 1952
left The last of the Brabham/Tauranac-inspired cars was the BT44 and this BT44B was the beginning of the Gordon Murray era
far left The Alfa Romeo-powered BT45B driven by John Watson in 1977, a season that saw the Anglo-Italian car come so close to success

workshops at Mays's home at Bourne in Lincolnshire. The name given to the resulting car was the British Racing Motor and, when the project was begun shortly after the war, much was expected of the cars. However, various bungles in the organization and design departments, as well as half-hearted support from the industry, resulted in the cars being raceworthy too late, after the Formula to which they had been built had been changed.

The original BRM was a highly supercharged 1½-litre 16-cylinder machine, and though the engine was very advanced and certainly the most powerful in its class, the chassis was not so advanced and at no time were the cars able to challenge the successful cars of the 1949–52 period. The noise from the exhausts of the V16-cylinder BRM will long live in history, for many tape recordings were made at the time. The engine ran to 11,000 rpm and more, and was certainly one of the most exciting-sounding engines ever to shatter the racing circuits, and well I remember the first private showing of this promising car on the desolate Folkingham Aerodrome in the winter of 1949.

An early P25 BRM 2½-litre driven by Mike Hawthorn at Aintree in 1956

The whole project failed to reach its goal mostly because the design and construction of the car was beyond the capabilities of the people concerned, but it was indeed a valiant, if somewhat misguided effort. After spending a fantastic amount of money collected from various firms connected with the motor industry, this communal idea was wound up and Alfred Owen, head of the Rubery Owen Group of Companies, agreed to buy the whole set-up and continue to finance the project on his own, keeping Mays and Berthon in charge, though not wholly in control. With the advent of the 2½-litre Formula in 1954, work was begun on a new and more simple car, using a 4-cylinder unsupercharged engine, and though this car showed promise at various times, even to winning the Dutch GP in 1959, it never achieved the success for which its backer hoped. Like many other racing firms, the BRM designers eventually followed the Porsche, Auto Union and Cooper lead in design and built a car with the engine behind the driver, instead of the long-adhered-to forward position. The prototype was tried out in 1959 and in 1960 the whole team of cars were built to this smaller, lighter and more compact design but, though able to challenge the opposition pretty frequently, they never scored any major victories. For the new Formula of 1½-litres, started in 1961, BRM continued with their rear-engine layout, with all-round independent suspension, and used a Coventry-Climax engine while they completed the design and building of new V8 engines for 1962. This latest BRM, as tried out experimentally in practice for the 1961 Italian GP, was surely one of the sleekest-looking and most compact cars they ever built; it was also the most successful car they ever built, winning the Manufacturers' Championship in 1962 with some excellent wins. Throughout the years of the 1½-litre Formula the V8 BRM was among the leading contenders, and a 2-litre version was very successful in the Tasman series, but when the Formula rules changed

The slim P261 BRM in 2-litre Tasman form driven by Graham Hill at Nurburgring in 1966

in 1966 they lost their grip on the situation and slid downhill again.

The new Formula was for 3-litre engines and BRM built another 16-cylinder engine that was as exciting and complex as the old original 16-cylinder, and about as unsuccessful. The cylinders were arranged in the form of a letter H lying on its side, with two crankshafts geared together. Although a large engine, it was surprisingly compact and tidy, and fitted neatly into the back of the new car. The chassis broke new ground in being an aluminium monocoque comprizing the front half of the car, the engine and gearbox forming the rear half, with the engine bolted to the bulkhead behind the cockpit. This form of construction, perfected by Lotus after BRM had first appeared with it, is now almost universal in racing-car design. The H-16 car was very fast on occasions but never really succeeded and it caused a major rift in the BRM management.

While the H-16 engine was going through its development problems a more straightforward V12 cylinder engine was designed and built, with a view to it being used for long-distance sports-car events. After an internal row the H-16 was scrapped and a new car built around the V12 engine and this was developed into quite a successful series of 3-litre cars that has carried them through the years of the 3-litre Formula to the present day.

Over the years in which BRM have diversified from pure GP cars they have been involved in various projects for other forms of racing for clients, such as the Le Mans cars using Rover gas turbine engines, brief sorties into Can-Am racing with Chevrolet-powered cars and long-distance sports cars for Matra, as well as building engines for the 1-litre Formula 2 racing. Since this diversification the management changed dramatically, ownership passing to the Stanley family, Mrs. Jean Stanley being Sir Alfred Owen's sister. With the advent of heavy sponsorship and advertising in racing in 1970, the BRM team were backed by the Yardley Cosmetics firm, wearing the livery of cosmetics rather than the traditional British Racing Green. Under the new Stanley regime the BRM fortunes wavered from complete success to utter failure, there being no continuity in their efforts, while financial backers have come and gone with increasing rapidity. The cars became Stanley-BRM and were no more successful than when they started as BRM in 1949.

Year: 1949/52
Model: Type 15 Formula 1
Engine: BRM
Number of cylinders: 16 in-vee
Bore and Stroke: 49·53 × 48·26 mm
Capacity: 1488 cc
Valves: Inclined overhead with four ohcs
Induction: Centrifugal supercharger
Wheelbase: 8 ft 2 in
Forward Speeds: 5
Front Suspension: Independent by trailing links and pneumatic struts
Rear Suspension: de Dion with pneumatic struts
Chassis Frame: Tubular
Maximum Speed: 180 mph

Year: 1955
Model: Type 25 Formula 1
Engine: BRM
Number of cylinders: 4
Bore and Stroke: 102·87 × 74·93 mm
Capacity: 2491 cc
Valves: Inclined overhead with two overhead camshafts
Induction: Two Weber carburettors
Wheelbase: 7 ft 6 in
Forward Speeds: 4
Front Suspension: Independent by double wishbones and pneumatic struts, later changed to coil springs
Rear Suspension: de Dion with transverse leaf springs later changed to coil springs
Chassis Frame: Tubular spaceframe
Maximum Speed: 165 mph

Year: 1962
Model: Type 56 Formula 1
Engine: BRM
Number of cylinders: 8 in-vee
Bore and Stroke: 68·1 × 50·8 mm
Capacity: 1482 cc
Valves: Inclined overhead with
four ohcs
Induction: Lucas fuel-injection
Wheelbase: 7 ft 5⅝ in
Forward Speeds: 5
Front and Rear Suspension:
Independent by double wishbones
and coil springs
Chassis Frame: Tubular space-
frame
Maximum Speed: 160 mph

The sleek but unsuccessful BRM
P180 of 1972 when the team had
Marlboro sponsorship

Year: 1971
Model: Type 160—Formula 1
Engine: BRM
Number of cylinders: 12 in-vee
Bore and Stroke: 74·6 × 57·2 mm
Capacity: 2999 cc
Valves: Four per cylinder with
two ohcs per bank
Induction: Lucas fuel-injection
Wheelbase: 8 ft 1 in
Forward Speeds: 5
Front Suspension: Double wishbones
and coil springs
Rear Suspension: Transverse link,
wishbone, radius rods, coil springs
Chassis Frame: Aluminium
monocoque with tubular engine bay
Maximum Speed: 180 mph

Brooke Special   England

H.L. Brooke of Coventry installed a supercharged MG Magnette engine in
a racing Riley chassis and began an intensive racing programme on the British
circuits in 1937. In 1938 he replaced the MG engine with various sizes of
6-cylinder unsupercharged Riley engines, depending on the available handicap, and also fitted André-Girling Riley independent front suspension to
the chassis. The car had originally been called an MG-Riley, but now became
the Brooke Special. In 1939 he replaced the Riley engine by a supercharged
1½-litre Alta engine and the car became known as the Alta-Brooke, but after
a few races in this form it was changed back to the Brooke Special as the
Alta engine was replaced by an ERA engine of 1½ litres.

After the war the car was greatly modified, being made much lower and it
ran in speed trials, usually without any bodywork. Leslie Brooke eventually

sold the car when he took up GP racing with an ERA and a Maserati, fitting a 1750-cc unsupercharged Riley engine back in the car before parting with it. Subsequently it won the Manx Cup race in the Isle of Man in 1948, driven by George Nixon and later was converted into a 2-seater sports car and still exists today.

Lesley Brooke selecting reverse gear on his Brooke Special after ramming the bank at Stadium Dip at the Crystal Palace in 1937. In this form the car has an MG engine in a Riley chassis

Year: 1938
Model: Special
Engine: Riley
Number of cylinders: 6
Bore and Stroke: 57·5 × 95·2 mm
Capacity: 1486 cc
Valves: Inclined overhead with pushrods
Induction: Carburettors

Wheelbase: 8 ft 3 in
Forward Speeds: 4
Front Suspension: Independent by transverse links, radius arms and coil springs
Rear Suspension: Semi-elliptic leaf springs
Chassis Frame: Channel-section
Maximum Speed: 125 mph

BRP England

The British Racing Partnership (BRP) was formed by Alfred Moss and Ken Gregory, father and manager, respectively of Stirling Moss. They began by borrowing cars from manufacturers, such as BRM and entered Stirling for some races in 1959 when he was not contracted to other teams, but one of the objects behind BRP was the encouragement of new young drivers. After running Cooper and Lotus cars they felt sufficiently knowledgeable to build their own car and in 1963 the first BRP was completed, powered by a 1½-litre V8 BRM engine and using a Colotti gearbox.

A team of two cars was run during 1964, with many ups and downs, but no real success, although the cars were quite competitive from the design point of view, following many Lotus principles, such as aluminium mono-coque chassis, and the all-round independent suspension that Lotus and Lola had made standard wear for Formula 1 cars.

In 1965 the BRP team became rather over-ambitious and built cars for the Indianapolis 500 Mile Race, using the 'off the shelf' racing Ford V8

Innes Ireland driving a BRP car with V8 BRM engine in practice for the 1963 German GP at the Nurburgring

engine. However, this project was really beyond the teams capabilities and was a final fling as far as car building was concerned. The following year saw the 3-litre Formula begin and anyone who did not have a close connection with an engine manufacturer, such as Maserati, Repco or Weslake, was out of the running during the first two seasons, until the Cosworth DFV became available. By this time the British Racing Partnership had closed down.

Year: 1964
Model: Formula 1
Engine: BRM
Number of cylinders: 8 in-vee
Bore and Stroke: 68·1 × 50·8 mm
Capacity: 1482 cc
Valves: Inclined overhead with four ohcs
Induction: Lucas fuel-injection
Wheelbase: 7 ft 7 in

Forward Speeds: 5
Front Suspension: Lower wishbones, upper rocker arm and inboard coil springs
Rear Suspension: Wishbone, link, radius rods and coil springs
Chassis Frame: Aluminium monocoque
Maximum Speed: 150 mph

Bugatti

France

Italian-born Ettore Bugatti, resident in France, had his entry for the 1901 Paris–Madrid race turned down as it was thought that his car was too low and did not afford the driver sufficient visibility over the engine! After doing design work for other manufacturers Bugatti raced a tiny 1300-cc 4-cylinder, single-ohc car in the 1911 *Formule Libre* GP, against rivals of vast size, finishing second to a 10½-litre Fiat.

In 1922 he reappeared in racing, at the Grand Prix de l'ACF at Strasbourg, with a team of 8-cylinder, single-ohc cars with three valves per cylinder, two inlet and one exhaust. The body was unique in being of circular section, ending in a tubular tail like a jet-pipe. From this date Bugatti produced a continual flow of racing cars, both for his own racing team and for sale to customers. In 1923 the same basic 8-cylinder engine was used in his aerodynamic 'tank' racing cars, with all-enveloping bodywork. He also made a special 'Indianapolis' version with narrow single-seater bodywork, but this was out of series and was not followed up in his subsequent designs. However, in 1924 he started a line of GP cars that was to become 'classic', the first being the Type 35, a 2-litre unsupercharged 8-cylinder of graceful proportions, with the now well-known Bugatti horseshoe radiator. The bodywork was 2-seater width, as mechanics were being carried, and had a pointed tail that still delights today. The wheels were patent Bugatti, of aluminium with integral brake-drum, and the suspension was by semi-elliptic springs passing through the tubular front axle beam, and reversed quarter-elliptic springs at the rear.

There was a series of Type 35 Bugattis, following this first model:

Type 35 GP 2-litre unsupercharged, 1924.

Type 35A Modified GP 2-litre unsupercharged, 1924.

Type 35C GP 2-litre supercharged, 1926.

Type 35T GP 2·3-litre unsupercharged, 1926.

Type 35B GP 2·3 litre supercharged, 1926.

Outwardly all these cars looked alike, and they all had single-ohc 8-cylinder engines, the 2-litre being 60×88 mm, the 2·3-litre 60×100 mm. In 1926, for the 1½-litre Formula, Bugatti built the Type 39, an 8-cylinder of 60×66 mm. For a long while Bugatti used two carburettors on his 8-cylinder engines, but in 1926 a Roots-type supercharger was mounted on the right-hand side

left The classic GP Bugatti in its purest form – the 'twin-cam' Type 51

right Charlie Martin rounding a corner in the 1935 Mannin Moar in the Isle of Man in his Type 59 Bugatti

of the engines of both 35 and 39 models, the latter being known as the 39A. Similarly he supercharged his 4-cylinder 1½-litre, The Type 37, or 'poor man's Grand Prix Bugatti', these being similar in chassis design to the 35 but having wire-spoke wheels in place of the alloy ones. The Type 35 and 39 Bugattis continued to win races against more powerful rivals by reason of superior handling characteristics, being easy and light to drive. However, a lot of Bugatti victories were hollow ones, being achieved in 1928/29 when other makes had withdrawn from racing and there were quite a lot of 'Bugatti only' races, which his cars could hardly help winning.

In 1931 Bugatti built his first twin overhead camshaft, inclined valve, GP engine, the Type 51. Still an 8-cylinder and basically the same as the Type 35, this new Bugatti was able to challenge all-comers, and a 1½-litre version, the 51A, was equally successful. He also built a fantastic 4·9-litre version for *Formule Libre* racing. Before this step forward in design Bugatti built an experimental 4-wheel-drive racing car, mainly for hill-climbs, and though it showed great promise he did not continue with the development of the car. For the 750 kilogramme Formula in 1934 Bugatti started with an entirely new design, which actually appeared as a 2·8-litre car in 1933. During 1934 they were enlarged to 3·3-litre and known as the Type 59—Bugatti's most elegant creation. It was a supercharged 8-cylinder of 72 × 100 mm with two ohc with the driver sitting low alongside the propellor shaft, in a 2-seater-width body. It had many innovations, such as a starting handle in the left-hand side of the chassis, turning the crankshaft by bevel gearing, wheels with radial spokes of very thin wire, the drive being taken by serrated teeth between the rim and the brake drum, and reversed quarter-elliptic springs at the rear, with non-independent front end. This was really the beginning of the end of Bugatti as a power in GP racing. The car could not combat the German teams, and from 1935 to 1939 the Bugatti works team made sporadic attempts at GP racing but none were successful. He kept his name and dignity by turning to sports-car racing with the Type 59 cars, fitting them with all-enveloping bodywork. In 1935 he produced a 3·8-litre engine and the following

year a 4·7-litre, always adhering to the straight-8 principle. The 4·7-litre car was a pure single-seater with the driver centrally placed, and for the 3-litre Formula in 1938 he produced another single-seater straight-8, but adhering to his obsolete leaf spring suspension and rigid axles, and though attractive-looking the car was quite hopeless.

Bugatti made history again in 1945 when his works driver Jean-Pierre Wimille won the first post-war motor race, in the Bois-de-Boulogne in Paris, driving the old 4·7-litre *monoplace*, albeit against some pretty tired and second-hand opposition. In 1947 le Patron died, and though his son Roland carried on running the Molsheim factory it was the end of racing activities, until a remarkable resurgence in 1956. The factory suddenly produced two cars for the 2½-litre Formula, which were remarkable machines designated the Type 251. They had an 8-cylinder engine mounted transversely behind the driver, at a time when all contemporary cars were still front-engined. The chassis was a space-frame of small-diameter tubing and had de Dion axles front and rear, or rigid beam axles, whichever way you care to view de Dion. Trintignant drove one in the 1956 French GP at Reims, but it retired and went back to Molsheim and was never seen again, nor was much more heard about Bugatti and racing.

Maurice Trintignant testing the Bugatti Type 251 on the airfield at
Entzheim near the Bugatti factory in March 1956

Today there are many Bugattis racing in VSCC historic events and still making the glorious exhaust noises for which the GP cars from Molsheim were noted. The classic GP Bugatti has become much sought after and is now valued at vast sums of money, and in consequence there are many fakes being made, using original or newly-made parts. Many of the cars from the factory, including the two Type 251 cars were acquired by Fritz Schlumpf for his museum at Mulhouse, not far from Molsheim.

Year: 1926
Model: Type 35B
Engine: Bugatti
Number of cylinders: 8 in-line
Bore and Stroke: 60 × 100 mm
Capacity: 2270 cc
Valves: Vertical overhead with single overhead camshaft
Induction: Roots-type supercharger
Wheelbase: 7 ft 10½ in
Forward Speeds: 4
Front Suspension: Semi-elliptic leaf springs
Rear Suspension: Reversed quarter-elliptic leaf springs
Chassis Frame: Channel-section
Maximum Speed: 125 mph

Year: 1934
Model: Type 59
Engine: Bugatti
Number of cylinders: 8 in-line
Bore and Stroke: 72 × 100 mm
Capacity: 3257 cc
Valves: Inclined overhead with two ohcs
Induction: Roots-type supercharger
Wheelbase: 8 ft 10 in
Forward Speeds: 4
Front Suspension: Semi-elliptic leaf springs
Rear Suspension: Reversed quarter-elliptic leaf springs
Chassis Frame: Channel-section
Maximum Speed: 160 mph

Year: 1956
Model: Type 251
Engine: Bugatti
Number of cylinders: 8 in-line
Bore and Stroke: 75 × 68·8 mm
Capacity: 2430 cc
Valves: Inclined overhead with two ohcs
Induction: Four Weber double-choke carburettors
Wheelbase: 7 ft 2 in
Forward Speeds: 5
Front Suspension: de Dion with coil springs
Rear Suspension: de Dion with coil springs
Chassis Frame: Tubular space-frame
Maximum Speed: 145 mph

Challenger   England

Reg Parnell started building this car in 1939 as a GP contender as it looked as though the new Formula was to be for 1½-litre cars. The war put a stop to the project, though he finished the chassis and ran it once at Prescott hill-climb, using an ERA engine and gearbox. The tubular chassis had i.f.s. and de Dion rear end and was based on the Mercedes-Benz of the day, while the body was of typical GP design. The engine was planned to be a twin-ohc 6-cylinder based on Parnell's experience with a special MG Magnette engine. At first the car was called 'The Challenge', but later 'Challenger'.

Immediately after the war Parnell installed a 1927 Delage 1½-litre straight-8 engine and David Hampshire raced it for a short time, but the Challenger as such was never completed.

Year: 1939
Model: 'Voiturette'
Engine: Parnell
Number of cylinders: 6
Bore and Stroke: 66·75 × 71 mm
Capacity: 1492 cc
Valves: Inclined overhead with two ohcs
Induction: Supercharged

Wheelbase: 8 ft 6 in
Forward Speeds: 4
Front Suspension: Independent by double wishbones and coil springs
Rear Suspension: de Dion with torsion bars
Chassis Frame: Tubular
Maximum Speed: Unknown

David Hampshire with the Challenger in 1947 when it had a straight-8 Delage engine installed

Challenger-1 America

Until beaten by the Summers brothers' car 'Golden Rod', Mickey Thompson's Challenger-1 was the fastest automobile-engined car in the world. Powered by four Pontiac V8-cylinder engines driving all four wheels, it recorded an

Mickey Thompson in the cockpit of Challenger-1 in 1959, showing how the driver was positioned 'sling-shot' style behind the rear wheels

official two-way run at Bonneville of 362 mph. The only cars to have gone faster at the time were driven by aeroplane engines. In 1960 Thompson fitted each of the four engines with a supercharger, and in this form he attempted the record once more. After a one-way run of 406 mph, trouble prevented the return run and stopped him establishing a record.

Year: 1959/61	*Induction:* Four superchargers
Model: Record	*Wheelbase:* 9 ft 1 in
Engine: Pontiac	*Forward Speeds:* 3
Number of cylinders: 32 in four V8s	*Front Suspension:* None
Bore and Stroke: 103·2 × 101·6 mm	*Rear Suspension:* None
Capacity: 6784 cc each engine	*Chassis Frame:* Stressed-skin structure
Valves: Inclined overhead with pushrods	*Maximum Speed:* 400 mph

Chevron   England

After building specials for club racing, Derek Bennett, of Salford in Lancashire, built the first Chevron sports/racing car in 1965 and the following year moved into a factory in Bolton and went into production with the first model. Sports and GT racing cars followed and in 1967 he built his first single-seater, a Formula 3 car, known as the B7. All his car models were given the suffix B. The first F3 car was improved the following year and became the B9 which went into small-scale production. This was followed by an F2 version and in 1969 the B15 appeared which differed from previous models in having an aluminium monocoque centre cockpit section and a tubular frame at the rear to carry the engine and gearbox. In most cases Ford or Cosworth engines were used for the various Formulae.

The Chevron single-seaters were successful in all forms of small Formulae

A 1977 Chevron B40 with 4-cylinder BMW engine for Formula 2

racing and a continuous line of development has been followed. Engines vary according to the rules of any given Formula, and Formula 1 is about the only branch of single-seater racing that Chevron have not supplied a chassis for. Among the engines used, in conjunction with a Hewland final drive, are 4-cylinder Ford, Cosworth, BMW and Ferrari V6.

The Chevron designs are comparatively straightforward, offering uncomplicated servicing by the owner, and Derek Bennett has continued to be one of the major suppliers of racing cars, in spite of much opposition. They have built up a name for being functional and honest cars, very raceworthy and not absurdly expensive or unnecessarily sophisticated. For anyone contemplating starting single-seater racing the Chevron is one of the best makes on the market.

Year: 1977
Model: B40—Formula 2
Engine: BMW
Number of cylinders: 4
Bore and Stroke: 89·2 × 80 mm
Capacity: 1999 cc
Valves: Four per cylinder, two overhead camshafts
Induction: Fuel-injection
Wheelbase: 7 ft 7¾ in

Forward Speeds: 5
Front Suspension: Double wishbones and coil springs
Rear Suspension: Transverse link, wishbone, radius rods and coil springs
Chassis Frame: Aluminium monocoque with tubular engine bay
Maximum Speed: 165 mph

Chrysler America

The Chrysler Corporation did not support racing in a big way, but some special racing Chryslers were built for American track events, and some were occasionally seen competing in European road racing, but never very successfully. They were unusual in having hydraulically operated external-contracting brakes.

Raul Riganti of Argentina before the Indianapolis 500 Mile Race in 1933 in his racing Chrysler straight-8

Year: 1932
Model: Indianapolis
Engine: Chrysler
Number of cylinders: 8 in-line
Bore and Stroke: 85·7 × 127 mm
Capacity: 5863 cc
Valves: Overhead

Induction: Carburettors
Wheelbase: 8 ft 4 in
Forward Speeds: 3
Front and Rear Suspension:
Semi-elliptic leaf springs
Chassis Frame: Channel-section
Maximum Speed: 125 mph

Cisitalia
Italy

In 1946 two Italian racing drivers, Piero Taruffi and Piero Dusio, formed the Cisitalia Company in Turin and built some two dozen small racing cars to a very simple and inexpensive design. Races for these little D46 Cisitalia cars were held in Italy, often as an *hors-d'oeuvre* before a GP.

The cars had a multi-tube 'space-frame', then very advanced but later

The very advanced mid-engined Cisitalia GP car seen on its completion in 1949

almost universal, and Fiat front suspension by transverse leaf spring and wishbones. The Fiat rear axle was suspended on a combination of torsion bars and coil springs. A special Fiat 1100 production engine was used, giving 60 bhp at 5500 rpm, using a compression ratio of 9·5:1, and a 3-speed gearbox of Cisitalia manufacture. The cars followed the then conventional lines of having the engine in front of the driver, and were like little GP cars to look at.

In 1947 Dusio was approached by the Porsche Design Company of Gmund, as he was thinking in terms of a GP car. Young Ferry Porsche, son of the famous doctor, prepared the plans for a supercharged 1½-litre GP car and sent two Austrian engineers, Hruschka and Abarth to Turin to supervise the construction. Dusio envisaged building six cars. Known as the Porsche Type 360, the car would be considered revolutionary even today, with a space-frame, all-independent suspension, rear-mounted engine and 4-wheel-drive. The engine was a horizontally opposed 12-cylinder, each bank of six having two overhead camshafts and fed by its own vane-type supercharger.

The drive to the four wheels, from the 5-speed syncromesh gearbox mounted between the engine and the final drive unit, could be locked in two- or four-wheel-drive by a lever in the cockpit. There were fuel tanks on each side of the cockpit and the general appearance was that of a pre-war Auto-Union.

By the end of 1948 Dusio was in financial trouble, the project costing far more than anticipated, and though the first car was completed in 1949 it never ran. Cisitalia went broke and in 1950 Dusio went to the Argentine, taking the prototype Porsche Type 360 with him. A new company called Auto Motores Argentina (Autoar) was formed, which ran the car once and set up a local speed record at 144·7 mph but other than that nothing more was heard of it until the Porsche factory brought the car back to Europe. The apprentices of the Porsche works cleaned it up and in 1961 it was started up and driven round the factory grounds. It is still owned by the Porsche factory. In 1970 a collection of parts that comprised a second Type 360 were discovered in Switzerland, never having gone to the Argentine, and these were bought by Tom Wheatcroft. There were not enough parts to complete the second car, but the main essentials were there and a body was built from drawings supplied by Porsche. This second Type 360 in partially completed form is on view in the Donington Park Racing Car Museum and enables the visitor to inspect many details of the design of this remarkable car which was designed in 1947.

Year: 1947
Model: D46
Engine: Fiat
Number of cylinders: 4
Bore and Stroke: 68 × 75 mm
Capacity: 1089 cc
Valves: Ohv with pushrods
Induction: Carburettor
Wheelbase: 6 ft 6¾ in

Forward Speeds: 3
Front Suspension: Independent by transverse leaf spring and lower wishbones
Rear Suspension: Rigid axle on torsion bars and coil springs
Chassis Frame: Tubular space-frame
Maximum Speed: 105 mph

Year: 1949
Model: Type 360
Engine: Porsche-Cisitalia
Number of cylinders: 12 horizontally opposed
Bore and Stroke: 56 × 50·5 mm
Capacity: 1492 cc
Valves: Inclined overhead with two camshafts per bank
Induction: Two vane-type superchargers

Wheelbase: 8 ft 7½ in (2600 mm)
Forward Speeds: 5
Front Suspension: Independent by trailing arms and torsion bars
Rear Suspension: Independent by transverse links, radius arms and torsion bars
Chassis Frame: Tubular space-frame
Maximum Speed: Unknown

Connaught England

Started by Rodney Clarke and Mike Oliver, with financial backing by Kenneth MacAlpine, son of the building family, the Connaught was originally a 'one-off' special for MacAlpine to race. Initial experiments were made with a much-modified 1750 cc Lea-Francis engine, and this was developed by Connaught into a 2-litre racing engine. After the first promising single-seater it was natural that others should follow and gradually a Connaught racing team appeared. The A-type cars were for 2-litre Formula 2 racing, and used the Connaught-built Lea-Francis pushrod ohv engine, with ENV pre-selector gearbox, large-diameter tubular chassis frame, with i.f.s. by wishbones and torsion bars, and de Dion layout with torsion bars at the rear. The Connaught was quite a feature in Formula 2 in 1952/53, but somehow the team never achieved any major successes, always being down on power compared with their rivals, though the chassis and road-holding were as good as any.

The B-type Connaught was ready for the 1954 GP Formula, using a special $2\frac{1}{2}$-litre 4-cylinder twin-ohc Alta engine, designed and built in collaboration with Geoffrey Taylor. At first these cars had all-enveloping streamlined bodies, but these were abandoned in favour of conventional racing bodywork, from practical rather than technical reasons. The chassis and suspension were a natural development of the A-type and in 1955 one of these cars made history, by being the first British car to win a GP race since 1924, when Tony Brooks beat the Maserati team at Syracuse.

left Dennis Poore driving an A-type Connaught in 1953

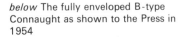

below The fully enveloped B-type Connaught as shown to the Press in 1954

The Connaught team were a strong force in GP racing in 1956, but did not achieve any more major successes, though they were well placed. A C-type car was begun in 1957 but never competed for a race, as the firm found the financial strain of racing more than it could stand and had to withdraw before the situation became desperate. MacAlpine had already given up racing himself, and had withdrawn his financial support, so the end of 1957 saw the whole Connaught team and equipment auctioned off, some of the cars still continuing to race, albeit unsuccessfully, in private owners' hands. Today there are still one or two Connaughts taking part in Historic racing which are a good example of the beginning of Britain's GP supremacy.

Year: 1950/53
Model: A-type
Engine: Lea-Francis
Number of cylinders: 4
Bore and Stroke: 79 × 100 mm
Capacity: 1960 cc
Valves: Inclined overhead with pushrods
Induction: Four Amal carburettors or Hilborn fuel-injection

Wheelbase: 7 ft 1 in
Forward Speeds: 4 ENV preselector
Front Suspension: Independent by double wishbones and torsion bars
Rear Suspension: de Dion with torsion bars
Chassis Frame: Tubular
Maximum Speed: 135 mph

Year: 1954
Model: B-type
Engine: Alta
Number of cylinders: 4
Bore and Stroke: 93·5 × 90 mm
Capacity: 2470 cc
Valves: Inclined overhead with two ohcs
Induction: Two double-choke Weber carburettors

Wheelbase: 7 ft 6 in
Forward Speeds: 4 ENV preselector
Front Suspension: Independent by double wishbones and coil springs
Rear Suspension: de Dion with torsion bars
Chassis Frame: Tubular
Maximum Speed: 155 mph

Connew   England

After working for a time at the John Surtees establishment, Peter Connew decided he would build a Formula 1 car himself. This he did in a small workshop in London's East End with the aid of two helpers, starting the project in 1970 and taking eighteen months to complete the first car. There was little finance available for this ambitious idea and a sponsor had to be found before a Cosworth DFV engine and Hewland gearbox could be installed in the monocoque chassis of conventional layout, but with unusual rear suspension with inboard-mounted spring units. The French driver François Migault brought some finance to the project in return for a drive, and the debut of what was actually the second car built, was eventually made in the British GP in 1972, but proved disastrous as the rear suspension was inadequate for the Brands Hatch circuit and the car was withdrawn after the first practice session.

This second car was modified the following month and entered for the Austrian GP, again with Migault as the driver. The car was unpopular in practice as the oil tank split and spread lubricant all round the circuit. However, it qualified, albeit in the back row of the starting grid, but managed only 22 laps before the rear suspension broke. That was the last seen of the F1 Connew in GP racing, though at the end of 1972 David Purley hired it for a Brands Hatch event, without much satisfaction. As the PC1B it reappeared in 1973 as a Formula 5000 car, with Chevrolet V8 power, but crashed and was not seen again.

François Migault driving the Connew PC2 in practice for the British GP at Brands Hatch 1972

Year: 1972
Model: PC1
Engine: Cosworth DFV
Number of cylinders: 8 in-vee
Bore and Stroke: 85·6 × 64·8 mm
Capacity: 2993 cc
Valves: 4 per cylinder. Two ohcs per bank
Induction: Lucas fuel-injection
Wheelbase: 8 ft 1 in
Forward Speeds: 5 Hewland DG300

Front Suspension: Independent by upper rocker-arm with inboard coil spring, lower wishbone
Rear Suspension: Independent, inboard coil springs operated by levers and rockers
Chassis Frame: Aluminium monocoque; engine a stressed member
Maximum Speed: 170 mph

Cooper-Alta   England

In the search for more performance than the Cooper-Bristol, the 4-cylinder 2-litre Alta racing engine was put into the Mark II chassis for 1953, to the special order of Peter Whitehead and Anthony Crook. The chassis was unchanged from the Bristol version, the Alta engine being mated to the Bristol gearbox. On the Whitehead car the use of two double-choke Weber carburettors in place of the normal twin SUs, meant having a curved frame tube on the left. A third car was built for Stirling Moss, using an ENV preselector gearbox, and tuned on nitro-methane, using SU fuel-injection, the Alta engine gave 186 bhp. At Monza it was as fast as the Italian cars, but the 15-in tyres could not stand the strain, and such high speeds showed up the deficiencies in the road-holding of the Cooper chassis.

Peter Whitehead's Mk II Cooper with 4-cylinder 2-litre Alta engine with stub exhaust pipes

Year: 1953
Model: Mark II
Engine: Alta
Number of cylinders: 4
Bore and Stroke: 83·5 × 90 mm
Capacity: 1970 cc
Valves: Inclined overhead with two ohcs
Induction: Carburettors or fuel-injection

Wheelbase: 7 ft 6 in
Forward Speeds: 4
Front and Rear Suspension: Independent by transverse leaf spring and wishbones
Chassis Frame: Tubular spaceframe
Maximum Speed: 160 mph

Cooper-Alta Special   England

When the idea of putting a 2-litre Alta engine into the Cooper-Bristol chassis was mooted. Stirling Moss decided to go one better and enlisted Ray Martin and Alf Francis to build a special car on the same principles. By the time they had made an improved chassis frame, double wishbone and coil spring front suspension and de Dion rear suspension there was little Cooper left. An Alta 4-cylinder engine and Alta gearbox were installed and Coopers made a special single-seater body. The car was built in twelve weeks and was just ready for Easter 1953. Due to this rush, it never received any serious testing or development work, and half-way through the season Stirling Moss abandoned it as it did not handle properly, mainly due to the chassis being too flexible. The engine and gearbox were taken out and put into a normal Formula 2 Cooper chassis.

The car lay idle for many years but was subsequently rebuilt with another Alta engine and today lives in a Scottish museum.

Stirling Moss in the abortive Cooper-Alta Special in 1953. It had Dunlop disc brakes and alloy wheels

Year: 1953
Model: F2 Special
Engine: Alta
Number of cylinders: 4
Bore and Stroke: 83·5 × 90 mm
Capacity: 1970 cc
Valves: Inclined overhead with two ohcs
Induction: Carburettors

Wheelbase: 7 ft 3 in
Forward Speeds: 4
Front Suspension: Independent by double wishbones and coil springs
Rear Suspension: de Dion with coil springs
Chassis Frame: Tubular space-frame
Maximum Speed: 145 mph

Cooper-Bristol   England

Built in 1952/3 for Formula 2 racing, this car was of very simple layout, using a sports Bristol engine and gearbox in a welded-up chassis frame developed from knowledge gained with Formula 3 cars. Early cars had a box-section chassis with tubular superstructure to carry the bodywork, while Mark II cars had a tubular space-frame. All models used transverse leaf springs front and rear, with tubular lower wishbones, giving independent wheel movement.

With 135 bhp in such a light car, easy to drive and consistent in its handling, the Cooper-Bristol was very fast round smooth circuits with lap speeds around the 80-mph mark. Mike Hawthorn used one of these cars as a stepping stone into the Ferrari team, his performances in 1952 being outstanding.

Although not a serious challenger to the Italian cars of the time, the Cooper-Bristol did provide some good racing at comparatively low cost, and the Bristol Car Division did a lot of development work on the 6-cylinder pushrod engine, which was derived from the pre-war BMW 328 engine, but it could never be considered a pure racing engine.

A number of cars can still be seen in action in Historic racing car events, though few of them are completely original. The Cooper-Bristol is a very easy car to reconstruct from new materials.

left Mike Hawthorn driving in the wet Belgian GP of 1952 with his Cooper-Bristol, identified at the time by the large bonnet-top air-intake

right The all-enveloping body on the rear-engined Cooper-Bristol derived directly from the Cooper sports car. It is seen in the paddock at Aintree in 1955

Year: 1952/3
Model: Formula 2
Engine: Bristol
Number of cylinders: 6
Bore and Stroke: 66 × 96 mm
Capacity: 1971 cc
Valves: Inclined overhead with cross pushrods
Induction: Three down-draught carburettors

Wheelbase: 7 ft 6 in
Forward Speeds: 4
Front and Rear Suspension: Independent by transverse leaf spring and lower wishbones
Chassis Frame: Mk I box-section; Mk II tubular space-frame
Maximum Speed: 140 mph

Cooper-Bristol (Rear-engined)   England

Inspired by Jack Brabham in 1955, this car began the long series of rear-engined Cooper cars that eventually had such a remarkable effect on all forms of racing. Basically a rear-engined sports-car chassis, the 6-cylinder Bristol engine and Cooper-Citroën gearbox were squeezed into the space available and the all-enveloping bodywork retained, minus lamps and road equipment, etc. It first appeared at Aintree for the British GP and, though never a serious contender for Formula 1 honours, it provided Coopers with an entry into Formula 1, and the Cooper-Climax which superseded it put them on the road to success. Although entered as a 2¼-litre Bristol unit, it was in fact a normal BS4 model 2-litre, giving 140 bhp.

Year: 1955
Model: Formula 1
Engine: Bristol
Number of cylinders: 6
Bore and Stroke: 66 × 96 mm
Capacity: 1971 cc
Valves: Inclined overhead with cross pushrods
Induction: Three down-draught carburettors

Wheelbase: 7 ft 5 in
Front and Rear Suspension: Independent by transverse leaf spring and wishbones
Chassis Frame: Tubular space-frame
Maximum Speed: 145 mph

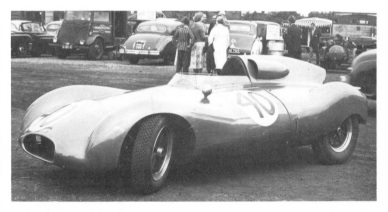

Cooper-Climax England

Having been encouraged by the rear-engined Cooper-Bristol and the rear-engined 1100-cc sports cars, it did not take Cooper long to build a single-seater with 1½-litre Coventry-Climax engine in the rear. In fact, it was ready before the 1½-litre Formula 2 was under way in 1957. From this it was a logical step to use larger engines, first of 2 litres, then 2·2 litres and eventually a full 2½-litre Coventry-Climax 4-cylinder. As the power increased so the car had to be made stronger, bigger, heavier and more complicated, until the 1960 Cooper-Climax GP car was quite a complex machine compared with the original Cooper-Climax.

The 2½-litre car won the Manufacturers' Championship in 1959 and 1960 and really convinced everyone of the desirability of a rear-engine layout. The same principles were retained for the 1½-litre Formula 1 of 1961/65, the Cooper cars starting with 4-cylinder Coventry-Climax engines, and in 1962 appearing with the first V8 engine from the Midlands firm. This compact V8 power unit, sold ready-to-race, powered the Cooper cars right through to the end of the 1½-litre Formula.

above Jack Brabham winning the 1959 Monaco GP with a 4-cylinder Cooper-Climax T51
below Bruce McLaren in a Cooper-Climax T60 in the 1964 German GP

Year: 1960
Model: T53
Engine: Coventry-Climax
Number of cylinders: 4
Bore and Stroke: 94 × 89·9 mm
Capacity: 2495 cc
Valves: Inclined overhead with two ohcs
Induction: Two double-choke Weber carburettors

Wheelbase: 7 ft 7 in
Forward Speeds: 5
Front Suspension: Independent by wishbones and coil springs
Rear Suspension: Independent by transverse leaf spring and wishbones
Chassis Frame: Tubular space-frame
Maximum Speed: 175 mph

Year: 1964
Model: T60
Engine: Coventry-Climax
Number of cylinders: 8 in-vee
Bore and Stroke: 63 × 60 mm
Capacity: 1494 cc
Valves: Inclined overhead with
two ohcs per bank
Induction: Down-draught
carburettors, later fuel-injection

Wheelbase: 7 ft 7 in
Forward Speeds: 6
Front and rear suspension:
Independent by wishbones and coil
springs
Chassis Frame: Tubular space-
frame
Maximum Speed: 160 mph

Cooper-ERA

England

The 1952 Formula 2 Cooper chassis being simple, light and very manageable,
it was used with numerous types of engine, and Peter Walker had a supercharged 2-litre ERA installed in one, for use in sprints and hill-climbs and
short *Formule Libre* races. It proved an interesting but short-lived experiment
and there were few events in which it could compete.

The 1952 Cooper with ERA 2-litre engine in the final stages of its construction

Year: 1952
Model: Formule Libre
Engine: ERA
Number of cylinders: 6
Bore and Stroke: 62·8 × 106·5 mm
Capacity: 1980 cc
Valves: Inclined overhead with
pushrods
Induction: Roots-type supercharger

Wheelbase: 7 ft 6 in
Forward Speeds: 4 ENV
preselector
Front and rear suspension:
Independent by transverse leaf
spring and wishbones
Chassis Frame: Box-section
Maximum Speed: 140 mph

Cooper-Maserati

Anglo–Italian

With the Cooper chassis not being designed and built for any specific engine unit, it was naturally the special-builder's delight, and for the 1960 Formula 1 season C.T. Atkins built a special car with a 2½-litre 4-cylinder Maserati engine installed in the rear. In 1961 the Italian Scuderia Centro-Sud, who had close connections with the Maserati firm, used 4-cylinder engines in 1961 Cooper chassis, both in 1½-litre and 2½-litre forms. These Maserati engines were basically sports-car units, but with Maserati the only difference between a sports engine and racing engine was that the sports one had provision for a starter and dynamo—a useful point when the 1961 Formula 1 rules called for a starter motor to be fitted to GP cars. They were true racing engines, all light-alloy, twin ohc, twin ignition system and twin double-choke Weber carburettors, and were adapted to connect to the Cooper gearbox/transmission unit.

Jochen Rindt in a works Cooper-Maserati V12 in 1966 during the Dutch GP

With these connections with the Modena firm it was no surprise when the Cooper factory came to an agreement to use V12 Maserati engines in their new cars for the 1966 Formula 1 of 3 litres. This engine had started life in 1957 as a 2½-litre unit for Formula 1, with a 3-litre version for sports-car racing. Maserati developed the 3-litre unit into a racing engine for Cooper, who installed it in a new aluminium monocoque chassis. The car was offered for sale to private owners but was not a great success, even though Maserati did a lot of development work on the engine, producing a special 3-valve-per-cylinder version. Cooper developed the chassis, producing a lower and lighter version, but the project came to an end by 1968 as the car was no longer competitive.

Year: 1961
Model: T51
Engine: Maserati
Number of cylinders: 4
Bore and Stroke: 81 × 72 mm
Capacity: 1484 cc
Valves: Inclined overhead with two ohcs
Induction: Two double-choke Weber carburettors
Wheelbase: 7 ft 7 in
Forward Speeds: 4
Front and rear suspension: Independent by double wishbones and coil springs
Chassis Frame: Tubular space-frame
Maximum Speed: 145 mph

Year: 1966
Model: T81
Engine: Maserati
Number of cylinders: 12 in-vee
Bore and Stroke: 70·4 × 64 mm
Capacity: 2989 cc
Valves: Inclined overhead with two ohcs per bank
Induction: Lucas fuel-injection
Wheelbase: 8 ft 2 in
Forward Speeds: 5 ZF
Front suspension: Independent by wishbone, rocker arm and coil spring
Rear suspension: Independent by wishbone, link and radius rods with coil springs
Chassis Frame: Aluminium monocoque
Maximum Speed: 175 mph

Cooper-Norton England

Having been one of the first to support 500 cc racing, which later became Formula 3, Cooper dominated this class right up to the end of its useful life. The first Coopers used JAP Speedway engines, but these were soon changed for the powerful 499 cc Manx Norton motor-cycle engine, driving by chain through a Norton gearbox to a chain final drive. The chassis started as two

Ivor Bueb in a Cooper-Norton in 1955. A scoop under the centre of the car deflected air up to the engine

Fiat 500 front-ends welded back-to-back, and this theme of all-round independent suspension was adhered to at all times, although the frame became a strong tubular affair.

Year: 1952	*Wheelbase:* 7 ft 3 in
Model: Formula 3	*Forward Speeds:* 4
Engine: Norton	*Front and Rear Suspension:*
Number of cylinders: 1 air-cooled	Independent by transverse leaf
Bore and Stroke: 79·62 × 100 mm	spring and wishbones
Capacity: 499 cc	*Chassis Frame:* Tubular space-
Valves: Inclined overhead with	frame
two ohcs	*Maximum Speed:* 120 mph
Induction: Amal carburettor	

Cosworth 4-W-D   England

As supplier of engines to most of the British Formula 1 teams, Keith Duckworth listened with interest to the rumblings heralding the building of 4-wheel-drive cars in 1968/69. Convinced that everyone was going to do it the wrong way he designed his own Cosworth 4-W-D car with the help of his design assistant Robin Herd (who later went to March Engineering). Whereas most 4-W-D designs used many existing parts and shapes, depending on the team, the Cosworth was a new concept in construction and shape, since there had been no previous Cosworth car to influence the design. It had the benefit of a one-off magnesium-block Cosworth DFV engine. Cosworth designed their own transmission and torque-split device, as well as new magnesium wheels with a single small nut fixing, that was later to appear on March cars. The engine was turned round 180-degrees to normal, coupled to a 6-speed gearbox situated just behind the driver's seat and the power shaft ran along

Mike Costin, the Cos of Cosworth, demonstrating the 4-wheel-drive Cosworth at Mallory Park in 1969

the right-hand side of the car to differentials front and rear, while disc brakes were all mounted 'inboard'. The chassis consisted of two aluminium sponsons, containing the fuel tanks, joined by a stressed-steel floor pan. The car was unusual in being very angular, and was of aluminium rather than fibreglass, with a flat wedge-shaped nose. Suspension fore and aft was by inboard coil springs operated by long rocker-arms which were themselves one leg of a wide-base wishbone.

One car was completed and parts for a second were made but never finished, and though the car was tested at Silverstone and entered for the 1969 British GP it was withdrawn before official practice began. There were problems with controlling the inner wheels spinning when cornering and the steering was heavier than was tolerable. Almost too soon Duckworth and his partner Mike Costin (Cos-Worth) abandoned this project without ever racing it and sold it to the Donington Collection of single-seater racing cars, complete with all the parts of the second car.

Year: 1969
Model: 4-W-D
Engine: Cosworth DFV
Number of cylinders: 8 in-vee
Bore and Stroke: 85·6 × 64·8 mm
Capacity: 2993 cc
Valves: 4 per cylinder. Two ohcs per bank
Induction: Lucas fuel-injection

Wheelbase: 7 ft 6 in
Forward Speeds: 6
Front and Rear Suspension: Independent by double wishbones with rocker-arm operation of inboard coil springs
Chassis Frame: Aluminium and steel structure
Maximum Speed: Unknown

Coyote   America

Texan racing driver A.J. Foyt was one of the last drivers to race successfully with the old-style front-engined 'roadster' USAC cars winning for the last time with one in 1964, but he had to give into the 'funny cars' as he termed them. These were the European-styled mid-engined cars introduced to the Indianapolis world by John Cooper and Jack Brabham in 1961, and later so successfully by Colin Chapman and Jimmy Clark with the Lotus-Ford V8. Foyt raced a Lotus to begin with but then modified it extensively to his own ideas, and ultimately produced an entirely new car along the same lines, that he called Coyote. He won the Indy 500 in 1967.

When the Ford (Detroit) Motor Company gave up producing and servicing the Indianapolis 4-ohc Ford V8 engine, Foyt took over the business at his Texas base, and later developed a turbo-charged version to combat the ever-successful Offenhauser 4-cylinder engine. Since that time he has raced a line of Coyote cars, powered by the turbo-charged Ford V8 engine, in all

USAC events, as well as supplying similar power units to other chassis constructors. A.J. Foyt and his Coyotes are still among the top runners in this form of American track-racing.

A.J. Foyt poses with his Gilmore Racing Team Coyote at Indianapolis in 1973

Year: 1973
Model: IV
Engine: Ford
Number of cylinders: 8 in-vee
Bore and Stroke: 95·5 × 45·7 mm
Capacity: 2619 cc
Valves: Inclined overhead with four ohcs
Induction: Turbo-chargers (two)
Wheelbase: 8 ft 8 in
Forward Speeds: 4—Hewland LG500

Front Suspension: Upper rocker arm with inboard coil spring, lower wishbone
Rear Suspension: Single top link, twin lower, double radius rods and coil springs
Chassis Frame: Aluminium monocoque
Maximum Speed: 215 mph

Cromard Special England

This was a one-off car developed from an early 6-cylinder twin-cam Amilcar, by Bob Spikins and Basil de Mattos, of Laystall Engineering, the name Cromard was derived from the firm's cylinder liner trade-mark. It was started in 1948 and each year, between racing, it was modified, first having a 1½-litre high-cam Lea-Francis engine replacing the Amilcar unit, and later a 1¾-litre Lea-Francis racing engine, which developed 140 bhp. The chassis was improved by the addition of Volkswagen trailing-link i.f.s. and swing-axle rear suspension, while the Amilcar gearbox was replaced by a preselector

ENV. Naturally it had a new body made for it. It was raced regularly until 1951, by which time it had served its useful life as a car for circuit racing. It still exists today and occasionally appears in VSCC meetings.

P.C.T. Clark driving the Cromard Special at Goodwood in 1951

Year: 1948/51
Model: Special
Engine: Lea-Francis
Number of cylinders: 4
Bore and Stroke: 75 × 100 mm
Capacity: 1767 cc
Valves: Inclined overhead with pushrods
Induction: Two carburettors

Wheelbase: 8 ft 0 in
Forward Speeds: 4
Front Suspension: Independent by trailing arms and torsion bars
Rear Suspension: Independent by swing axles and leaf spring
Chassis Frame: Tubular
Maximum Speed: 120 mph

Crosslé   Northern Ireland

John Crosslé started by building himself a Ford 10 special for the Irish 1172-cc Formula racing in 1957 and when he won the Ford Championship he soon had demands for similar cars from his friends. In 1961 he set up in business near Belfast and built racing-car chassis for Formula Junior with rear-mounted ohv Ford engines, and from these went on to build specials and one-off cars for a variety of racing activities, such as small-circuit racing and hill-climbs. Such specials varied in size and engine type from sv Ford 10 units to V8 Ford engines.

Business progressed steadily, with numerous exports to the USA for single-seater club racing, the chassis being a space-frame design. In 1969 he built cars for the Formula Ford Championship, in conjunction with C.T. Wooler Ltd on the engine tuning, and after a Crosslé won the Championship, production went on to Formula 3 and even Formula 2.

Still a small, almost one-man business, the Crosslé commands sufficient demand to keep the Northern Ireland factory very busy, with models for Formula Ford and Formula 2000.

The 1969 European Formula Ford Champion Crosslé driven by Gerry Birrell

Year: 1969
Model: 16F—Formula Ford
Engine: Ford
Number of cylinders: 4
Bore and Stroke: 81 × 77·6 mm
Capacity: 1598 cc
Valves: ohv pushrod operated
Induction: Carburettor
Wheelbase: 7 ft 4 in

Forward Speeds: 4
Front Suspension: Independent by wishbones and coil springs
Rear Suspension: Independent by links, radius rods and coil springs
Chassis Frame: Tubular space-frame
Maximum Speed: 130 mph

CTA-Arsenal   France

In 1946 the French *Centre d'Etudes Techniques de l'Automobile et du Cycle*, or CTA for short, decided to build a 'high-speed research vehicle' in the form of a 1½-litre GP car. Raymond Sommer was connected with the idea and the director of CTA put his department to work on the project, the Government giving permission for the car to be manufactured in the State Arsenal at Chatillon. The well-known designer Albert Lory was put in charge and the CTA–Arsenal was begun. In 1947 the first car was tested at Montlhéry and entered for the French GP at Lyons. It had a V8-cylinder engine, two ohcs to each bank, two-stage supercharging, dual ignition and developed 266 bhp at 7500 rpm. The chassis frame was of sheet steel in box-section form and suspension to all four wheels was independent by a curious system of vertical sliders and transverse links coupled to torsion bars. A 4-speed gearbox was used and the bodywork contained five separate fuel tanks in order to distribute the load.

The car was far from ready when it appeared at Lyons and at the start the clutch gave trouble and a half-shaft broke! A second car was completed and the two were entered for the 1948 French GP at Reims, but after practice both were withdrawn. That was the last seen of this expensive and extravagant piece of research, and CTA changed its name to *Union Technique de l'Automobile et du Cycle*, and got on with more mundane things. Eventually the Talbot-Lago firm bought the two cars but never did anything with them and today one of them resides within the French museum circuit, always being on view somewhere in France. It was to have been a fine GP car to carry the French racing blue, and on paper it was very impressive, but the whole project was far too complicated for those in charge.

Year: 1947
Model: Grand Prix
Engine: Albert Lory design
Number of cylinders: 8 in-vee
Bore and Stroke: 60 × 65·6 mm
Capacity: 1482 cc
Valves: Inclined overhead with four ohcs
Induction: Two-stage supercharging
Wheelbase: 8 ft 1 in
Forward Speeds: 4
Front and Rear Suspension: Independent by vertical sliders and torsion bars
Chassis Frame: Box-section
Maximum Speed: Unknown

Raymond Sommer leaving the pits in practice for the 1947 French GP at Lyons in the sleek-looking, but unsuccessful CTA-Arsenal

DAF   Holland

The DAF car and truck firm did not make a complete racing car to start with, but financed the building and running of a Formula 3 car based on a 1965 Brabham chassis, with Cosworth engine. They lengthened the frame and used the unique DAF belt transmission with fully-automatic operation and infinitely variable ratios. The system worked quite satisfactorily under racing conditions, the only drawback being a slight power loss and a weight handicap.

Sufficiently pleased with initial results they built their own chassis and ran a works team. Later they reverted to a proprietary chassis, buying Tecnos from Italy and using Holbay-Ford engines. After three years a halt was called to the activity and the sound of a Formula 3 engine at peak rpm while the DAF Variomatic transmission sorted the drive to the wheels, disappeared from the circuits.

Year: 1967
Model: F3
Engine: Ford
Number of cylinders: 4
Bore and Stroke: 80·1 × 48·4 mm
Capacity: 997 cc
Valves: Pushrod overhead
Induction: Carburettor
Wheelbase: 7 ft 11 in
Forward Speeds: DAF Variomatic transmission
Front suspension: Double wishbones and coil springs
Rear Suspension: Wishbone, link, radius rods and coil springs
Chassis Frame: Tubular space-frame
Maximum Speed: 130 mph

Jack Brabham with the DAF Variomatic belt-driven Brabham Formula 3 car in 1965

DB   France

The DB originated in 1948 when Charles Deutsch and René Bonnet started building specials for sports-car racing. They tried numerous power units and finally settled on the Panhard flat-twin, air-cooled 850-cc engine, and with it

The supercharged 750-cc DB with fwd, seen at the pits before the 1955 Pau GP

the fwd transmission and suspension. After many years of racing and manufacturing sports cars under the name D.B. Panhard, the Panhard part was dropped, though the basic idea did not change.

In 1955 Bonnet thought he would try his hand at Formula 1 racing, having been building 500-cc DBs for Formula 3, and a 'circus' of little 850-cc single-seaters called Monomills. He made a 750-cc version of the Panhard flat-twin and fitted it with a Roots-type supercharger, thus qualifying under the Formula 1 rules to run with the unsupercharged $2\frac{1}{2}$-litre cars. Two of these blown 750s, which were in reality enlarged Monomills, ran at Pau. They were hopeless, so Bonnet returned to sports-car racing, where he was much more successful.

Year: 1955
Model: Formula 1
Engine: Panhard
Number of cylinders: 2 air-cooled opposed
Bore and Stroke: 79·6 × 75 mm
Capacity: 748 cc
Valves: Inclined overhead with pushrods
Induction: Roots supercharger

Wheelbase: 6 ft $7\frac{3}{4}$ in
Forward Speeds: 4
Front Suspension: Independent by transverse leaf spring and wishbones, incorporating fwd
Rear Suspension: Independent by trailing arms and torsion bars
Chassis Frame: Box-section
Maximum Speed: 110 mph

Delahaye   France

Monsieur Delahaye started building cars at Tours in 1894, shortly after the inaugural motoring competition, the timed run from Paris to Rouen. It was his intention to enter the 1895 race from Paris to Bordeaux and back, but his car was not ready, and it was 1896 before the first Delahaye cars appeared on a starting-line. These primitive twin-cylinder cars were regular competitors until the turn of the century, and 4-cylinder Delahaye cars raced until 1902. After that the name disappeared from the circuits until a sports-car revival in France in 1936, by which time the firm had combined with Delage.

In 1937 they built a rather nice pushrod V12 cylinder car of $4\frac{1}{2}$ litres unsupercharged, which could run as a sports car or a racing car, and an energetic racing programme was instigated by the then director of the firm, Charles Weiffenbach. The 12-cylinder achieved the distinction of winning a prize of a million francs offered by the Automobile Club of France for the GP Formula car averaging the highest speed over 200 kilometres on the Montlhéry road circuit before the end of August 1937. Running stripped the V12 Delahaye, with Rene Dreyfus driving, averaged 146·654 kph on 27 August 1937, beating the Bugatti contender.

Gianfranco Comotti during practice for the German GP in 1938, with the V12 *monoplace* Delahaye

Jean François, the designer of the V12 created a single-seater version for GP racing in 1938, the Formula allowing a top limit of 4½-litres unsupercharged, and though competing regularly the *monoplace* Delahaye was no match for the supercharged 3-litre cars of Germany and Italy. In design features the *monoplace* was very advanced, having a de Dion axle location by twin radius rods each side (something normally attributed to Ferrari in 1950) and twin plugs to each cylinder, while the fuel tanks were within the wheelbase, there being no overhung weight behind the rear axle. A low propshaft line was achieved by having reduction gears in the rear hubs, so that the half-shafts were very low and below the wheel centres. The engine gave 250 bhp at 6000 rpm.

It re-appeared briefly after the war with the rear axle converted to a conventional layout on semi-elliptic springs, but then disappeared.

Year: 1938
Model: Type 145 'Monoplace'
Engine: Delahaye
Number of cylinders: 12 in-vee
Bore and Stroke: 75 × 84·7 mm
Capacity: 4490 cc
Valves: Inclined overhead with pushrods
Induction: Down-draught carburettors

Wheelbase: 9 ft 6 in
Forward Speeds: 4 Cotal electric
Front Suspension: Independent by transverse leaf spring and links with radius rods
Rear Suspension: de Dion with transverse leaf spring
Chassis Frame: Box-section
Maximum Speed: 155 mph

Derby-Maserati

Franco–Italian

This was a 'one-off' special from the hands of Douglas Hawkes and the French Derby factory in 1935. The chassis had all-independent suspension by swinging arms and leaf springs, and used a Derby fwd mechanism and

The Derby-Maserati seen in an Historic race at Brands Hatch post-war

gearbox. Into the very narrow chassis frame was installed a 4C Maserati engine, a 1½-litre 4-cylinder supercharged, mounted back-to-front, to couple-up with the fwd. It was run at Brooklands and in one or two Continental races, driven by Mrs. Gwenda Stewart, but without success and was notable for the strange attitude of the wheels when cornering, as they all leant outwards. A few years ago it was run in VSCC Historic events, but then passed into the Donington Racing Car Museum, where it can now be seen.

Year: 1935
Model: 'Voiturette'
Engine: Maserati
Number of cylinders: 4
Bore and Stroke: 69 × 100 mm
Capacity: 1496 cc
Valves: Inclined overhead with two ohcs
Induction: Supercharged
Wheelbase: 8 ft 11 in

Forward Speeds: 4 Derby
Front Suspension: Independent by wishbones and transverse leaf spring with fwd
Rear Suspension: Independent by half-axles and transverse leaf spring
Chassis Frame: Channel section
Maximum Speed: 125 mph

Derby-Miller

Franco–American

Basically a fwd Miller 91, the Derby-Miller was tuned and developed by Douglas Hawkes especially for track-racing at Brooklands and record attempts at Montlhéry. It was driven by Mrs. Gwenda Stewart (later Mrs. Hawkes) and she held the lap record at Montlhéry with it at 147·79 mph and in 1935 the Brooklands Ladies' lap record at 135·95 mph. Hawkes was connected with the Derby factory in Paris during the mid-thirties and the car was maintained and developed there, hence the Derby part of its new name. It went to Northern Ireland after the war and then disappeared, though it is said to be in America.

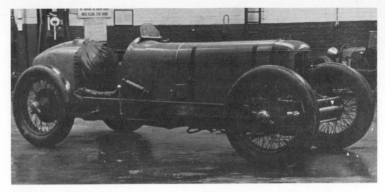

The Derby-Miller photographed in Bobby Baird's garage in Belfast after the war

Year: 1930
Model: Miller 91
Engine: Miller
Number of cylinders: 8 in-line
Bore and Stroke: 59 × 76·2 mm
Capacity: 1667 cc
Valves: Inclined overhead with two ohcs
Induction: Centrifugal supercharger

Wheelbase: 8 ft 4 in
Forward Speeds: 3
Front Suspension: de Dion by double quarter-elliptic springs, with fwd
Rear Suspension: Semi-elliptic leaf springs
Chassis Frame: Channel-section
Maximum Speed: 150 mph

Derrington-Francis   Anglo–Italian

With finance from Vic Derrington, the English tuning expert, the well-known racing mechanic Alf Francis, acquired the remains of the ill-fated ATS Formula 1 venture. From the parts he built up a new car around a shorter-

Alf Francis warming up the reborn ATS in Derrington-Francis form for practice at the 1964 Italian GP at Monza

wheelbase tubular-chassis frame, with Colotti gearbox mounted conventionally behind the rear axle. The V8 engine underwent a lot of work and the revised and much-improved car appeared at the Italian GP in 1964 driven by the Portuguese driver Mario Cabral. It proved to be little more successful than the original ATS, retiring with engine trouble.

Year: 1964
Model: F1
Engine: ATS
Number of cylinders: 8 in-vee
Bore and Stroke: 66 × 54·6 mm
Capacity: 1494 cc
Valves: Inclined overhead with two ohcs per bank
Induction: Lucas fuel-injection
Wheelbase: 7 ft 1¼ in

Forward Speeds: 6 Colotti (behind axle line)
Front Suspension: Independent by wishbones and coil springs
Rear Suspension: Independent by transverse links, radius rods and coil springs
Chassis Frame: Tubular space-frame
Maximum Speed: 140 mph

De Tomaso   Italy

The Argentinian driver Alessandro de Tomaso made his home in Modena while he was in Europe racing Maserati and Osca sports cars, and after abandoning active competition he continued to live in Italy, building racing cars for sale to amateur drivers. After one or two prototype attempts, he produced a 1½-litre Formula 1 car in 1961 that was available with either a 4-cylinder OSCA engine, or a bored-out Alfa Romeo Giulietta engine, with special twin-plug cylinder head. The chassis was built from small tubes, on current English racing-car practice, with double-wishbone and coil-spring suspension all round. Disc brakes and Italian cast-alloy wheels were fitted, and the 5-speed gearbox was a de Tomaso design, manufactured in Italy.

The design of the car was deliberately uncomplicated as it was the intention to provide a Formula 1 car at a fair price for a beginner, not to produce a car that would beat Ferrari, Lotus, Cooper, etc. With a limited number of 4-cylinder cars built, De Tomaso turned his attention to a more complicated car for his own use, and this had a flat 8-cylinder engine of his own design for the 1½-litre Formula. Though it appeared once or twice it was never a success as finances never allowed for its proper development.

He built cars with a remarkable cast-magnesium monocoque for Indianapolis with Ford racing engines, to special order, but without success and made forays into other racing categories, including Formula 1 in 1970 when he produced cars for Frank Williams, using Cosworth DFV engines and Hewland gearboxes. The cars were orthodox 'British Kit Car' assemblies, inspired, like so many Formula 1 cars, by the Lotus 49 of 1967. This activity lasted for

Piers Courage driving a De Tomaso-Cosworth V8 in 1970 for the Frank Williams team

one season only and then De Tomaso concentrated on production GT cars and industrial projects. Today he controls a major share of the specialized motor industry in Italy, as well as the motor-cycle industry.

Year: 1961
Model: F1
Engine: OSCA (or Alfa Romeo)
Number of cylinders: 4
Bore and Stroke: 78 × 78 mm
Capacity: 1490 cc
Valves: Overhead with two ohcs
Induction: Two double-choke Weber carburettors

Wheelbase: 7 ft 5¾ in
Forward Speeds: 5
Front and Rear Suspension:
Independent by double wishbones and coil springs
Chassis Frame: Tubular space-frame
Maximum Speed: 145 mph

Year: 1970
Model: Type 38 Formula 1
Engine: Cosworth DFV
Number of cylinders: 8 in-vee
Bore and Stroke: 85·6 × 64·8 mm
Capacity: 2993 cc
Valves: 4 per cylinder, 4 ohcs
Induction: Lucas fuel-injection
Wheelbase: 7 ft 11 in
Forward Speeds: 5 Hewland

Front Suspension: Independent by wishbones and coil springs
Rear Suspension: Independent by transverse link, wishbone, radius rods and coil spring
Chassis Frame: Aluminium monocoque with cast-magnesium centre bulkhead; engine a stressed member
Maximum Speed: 175 mph

Dommartin   France

This was an abortive attempt by M. Emile Petit to revive his 8-cylinder SEFAC racing car in 1948. He proposed to use desmodromic valve gear and run the enlarged engine in unsupercharged form. It existed, inasmuch as the SEFAC was still in one piece, but it never raced (see SEFAC).

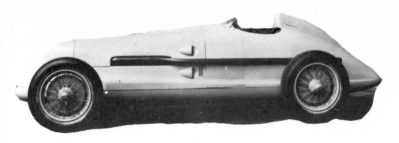

The Dommartin (nee SEFAC) seen on its brief release to the Press in 1948

Duesenberg America

The Duesenberg brothers were pioneers of the in-line 8-cylinder engine, their first car of this type running in the 1919 Indianapolis race. In 1921 they made history when Jimmy Murphy won the French GP at Le Mans, outdriving all the European aces. After that the Duesenberg firm concentrated on luxury cars and racing cars for American oval track racing, being extremely successful at Indianapolis and throughout the United States with their 8-cylinder cars.

In the early 1930s a consortium of businessmen commissioned 'Skinny' Clemons to build them some Indianapolis cars and having served his time with Harry Miller, the resulting $4\frac{1}{2}$-litre engine followed Miller principles. Clemons enlisted the aid of Augie Duesenberg on the project, as brother Fred had forsaken racing and was concentrating on touring cars, and the twin-cam straight-8 was installed in a Duesenberg 91 chassis. In 1933 Count Trossi, who was President of the Scuderia Ferrari, ordered one of these cars for European road racing, having been impressed by the speed of the Indianapolis cars and when the car arrived at Monza, finished in Italian racing red, it looked like an American version of a 'monoposto' Alfa Romeo. It ran only once in Italy, at Monza and then Trossi lent it to Whitney Straight who ran it at Brooklands, lapping at 138·34 mph but the narrow, whippy, chassis frame made it almost uncontrollable. Jack Duller bought it from the Trossi syndicate and it spent the remainder of its pre-war days at Brooklands, being modified in many small ways in an effort to try and improve its inadequate handling characteristics. Though it was an active competitor on the Brooklands Outer Circuit it never went quite as fast as when Whitney Straight drove it.

After the war the engine was taken out and put into an Emeryson Special, while the chassis had a Ford V8 engine installed and the car ran in speed trials. Engine and car have now been re-united.

Year: 1933
Model: Wonder Bread Special
Engine: Clemons
Number of cylinders: 8 in-line
Bore and Stroke: 88·4 × 89 mm
Capacity: 4376 cc
Valves: Inclined overhead with two ohcs
Induction: Two carburettors
Wheelbase: 8 ft 3½ in
Forward Speeds: 3
Front and Rear Suspension: Semi-elliptic leaf springs
Chassis Frame: Channel-section
Maximum Speed: 145 mph

R.L. Duller in the Duesenberg leaping the famous bump on the Brooklands Members banking in 1938

Eagle

America

After driving for numerous European GP teams—notably Ferrari, BRM and Brabham—Dan Gurney set out to build and race his own cars. He had already started a firm in California, under the name All American Racers, to operate cars in USAC oval-track racing, and in 1965 Anglo-American Racers was formed in England to run a Formula 1 programme. A universal chassis had been designed to accept the 4-ohc Ford Indy engine or a Formula 1 engine, and for the latter category Gurney commissioned Weslake Engineering to design and build a 3-litre V12 engine. The two sides of AAR ran concurrently, the cars being named Eagle, and in 1967 Gurney achieved the first of his ambitions when he won the Belgian GP at Spa in his own car.

In USAC racing the Eagle-Fords were proving real competitors and sales

Bruce McLaren 'guesting' for the Gurney Eagle team in the 1967 French GP with the first of the V12-engined cars

were strong, while another activity was in SCCA Formula 5000 racing. The Californian branch of AAR was fast-growing and profitable, whereas the English branch was struggling against strong opposition, and suffering from divided interests. In 1968 Gurney closed down Anglo-American Racers and concentrated on his Californian business. His burning ambition was to win the Indianapolis 500 Mile Race and though an Eagle won it in 1968, Dan himself was 2nd, and 2nd again in 1969. The 4-cam Ford engine had been replaced by the more powerful turbo-charged Meyer-Drake Offenhauser 4-cylinder and Eagle cars were in profusion in the USAC oval-track racing; by 1970 there were 10 in the 33 car starting list, and Gurney himself finished 3rd using a stock-block pushrod Ford V8 engine. It was to be his last competitive year and from then on Dan Gurney, as President of AAR Inc., concentrated on running the firm and managing the works team.

Success has continued to come the way of the Eagles, and in 1972 Bobby Unser made fastest Indy qualifying speed at 195·940 mph, while the following year he turned a lap at the Texas Speedway at 212·766 mph, to set up a new closed-circuit record. He won the Indianapolis 500 for Eagle in 1975 and the Gurney Eagles continue to be one of the top-runners in USAC oval-track racing.

Year: 1967
Model: T2G Formula 1
Engine: Gurney Weslake
Number of cylinders: 12 in-vee
Bore and Stroke: 72·8 × 60·3 mm
Capacity: 2997 cc
Valves: Inclined overhead, four per cylinder, with two ohcs per bank
Induction: Lucas fuel-injection
Wheelbase: 8 ft 0½ in

Forward Speeds: 5-Hewland
Front Suspension: Independent by lower wishbone and upper rocker arm operating inboard coil spring
Rear Suspension: Independent by lower reversed wishbone, transverse link, radius rods and coil spring
Chassis Frame: Aluminium monocoque
Maximum Speed: 185 mph

Dan Gurney in the Eagle-Ford V8 with which he finished 2nd in the 1968 Indianapolis 500 Mile Race after qualifying at 166.512 mph

Year: 1973
Model: Indianopolis
Engine: Meyer Drake Offenhauser
Number of cylinders: 4
Bore and Stroke: 111·1 × 67·3 mm
Capacity: 2611 cc
Valves: Inclined overhead with two ohcs
Induction: Turbo-charged
Wheelbase: 8 ft 6 in
Forward Speeds: 4-Weismann transaxle

Front Suspension: Upper rocker arm with inboard coil spring unit, lower wishbone
Rear Suspension: Single top link, double lower links, double radius rods and coil spring
Chassis Frame: Aluminium monocoque
Maximum Speed: 210 mph

Elva

England

The small Elva company was based on the Sussex coast, and run by Frank Nichols, who started by building sports/racing cars of typical post-war design, using proprietary parts in a light chassis frame. The name Elva was derived from the French *elle va* (slang for 'she goes'), and Nichols made quite a good business out of building and selling sports cars, mostly for competition work. When Formula Junior was introduced in 1960 his was one of the first British cars to take part, using a highly tuned German DKW 2-stroke engine in a narrow single-seater version of the sports cars. Being first off the mark, the DKW-Elva gained some successes, but was soon over-run by the rear-engined brigade. He followed this trend and put the DKW engine behind the driver and later changed to BMC and Ford power units in the search for more reliable power.

The chassis and suspension followed contemporary design—in line with such makes as Lotus, Lola and Gemini—and the Elva was quite popular in the early years of the Formula Junior, until Nichols concentrated on sports and GT cars and finally sold his firm to the Trojan group.

Elva Formula Junior car in action in 1960

Year: 1960
Model: Formula Junior
Engine: DKW
Number of cylinders: 3
Bore and Stroke: 74 × 76 mm
Capacity: 986 cc
Valves: 2-stroke porting
Induction: Carburettors
Wheelbase: 7 ft 5 in

Forward Speeds: 4
Front Suspension: Independent, wishbones and coil springs
Rear Suspension: Independent, wishbones, radius arms and coil springs
Chassis Frame: Tubular space-frame
Maximum Speed: 110 mph

Emeryson Special
England

Building specials runs in the Emery family, for 'Pa' Emery was building them pre-war, and in 1946 son Paul helped him build one of the first post-war specials. This was a chassis of their own design with i.f.s. from a Singer saloon, rear independent suspension of their own manufacture, using torsion bars, and a two-stage supercharged Lagonda Rapier 1100-cc engine driving through an ENV gearbox—a true special and the result of the efforts of Emery and his son, hence the name Emeryson. Paul Emery continued to build specials and kept the name. In 1947 the Emeryson Rapier was rebuilt to take the 4½-litre straight-8 engine from the Brooklands Duesenberg. This was followed by a fwd 500-cc Formula 3 car which went into limited production, but then another one-off car was built, this time for Paul himself. It used an Alta engine at first, but later was rebuilt with a 2·4 Jaguar engine. The rear-engined era saw Emery with a Connaught-powered car and in 1961 he built a number of fairly conventional F1 cars with Maserati 4-cylinder and Coventry-Climax 4-cylinder engines and Colotti gearboxes. A team of these cars was sold and became the basis for the Scirocco racing car.

For financial reasons Emery has always had to improvise with existing components, but this has never prevented him from producing some ingenious

Paul Emery and Bobby Baird stand behind the Duesenberg-engined Emeryson in front of the pits at Jersey in 1948

results. The Rapier engine he fitted with two-stage supercharging, he used fuel-injection on his Jaguar engine by modifying a diesel injector pump, he concocted a twin-engined car with a Coventry-Climax engine back and front, with 4-w-d and he was early in the field with glass-fibre petrol tanks and bodywork. In recent years he has been competing in midget-car racing with a car powered by a Hillman Imp engine. Paul Emery is one of the more ambitious and brighter people in the amateur world.

Year: 1947/48
Model: 1100
Engine: Lagonda Rapier
Number of cylinders: 4
Bore and Stroke: 62 × 90 mm
Capacity: 1098 cc
Valves: Inclined overhead with two ohcs
Induction: Two-stage supercharging
Wheelbase: 8 ft 4 in

Forward Speeds: 4 ENV preselector
Front Suspension: Independent by trailing arms and coil springs
Rear Suspension: Independent by fabricated forward-facing arms and transverse torsion bars
Chassis Frame: Tubular
Maximum Speed: 130 mph

Year: 1961
Model: Formula 1
Engine: Coventry-Climax
Number of cylinders: 4
Bore and Stroke: 81·9 × 71·1 mm
Capacity: 1498 cc
Valves: Inclined overhead with two ohcs
Induction: Two double-choke Weber carburettors

Wheelbase: 7 ft 4 in
Forward Speeds: 5 Colotti
Front suspension: Double wishbones and coil springs
Rear Suspension: Wishbone, links, radius rods and coil springs
Chassis Frame: Tubular space-frame
Maximum Speed: 145 mph

Mike Spence driving an Emeryson-Climax Formula 1 car at Silverstone in 1961

Ensign   England

Morris Nunn, as his name suggests, came from a motor industry background in the Midlands and during the late sixties he raced very successfully in Formula 3, graduating to the Lotus team in 1969. The following year he retired from competitive driving and started to build his own Formula 3 car, which he called the Ensign (N-sign). After running a Formula 3 team of these

Regazzoni in Ensign MN06 at the Spanish GP 1977

cars for various sponsors he set his sights on Formula 1. One of his Formula 3 drivers was Rikki von Opel, a rich young man who wanted to try his hand at GP racing, so he financed the building of a Formula 1 Ensign around the standard Cosworth DFV/Hewland package. This was completed in 1973 and was of striking appearance, with clean aerodynamic lines, but von Opel was not really competent enough to do it justice. Early in 1974 von Opel withdrew, but Nunn continued with MN01 and found other drivers and finance, carrying on into 1975 with money from a Dutch firm. He built two more cars, and for 1976 completed a brand new design, N-176 in the series. This car, MN05, he ran from his own resources with limited support from outside. MN04 passed to the Dutch firm of HB Alarm Systems and was renamed the Boro by the owners, the brothers Hoogenboom.

Of simple and straightforward construction, light and uncomplicated, the Ensign proved competitive, if not an actual winner, and the 1976 car had special front brakes with calipers fore and aft of each disc, which soon popularized this feature among other constructors. In the right hands the Ensign was capable of keeping up with the pacemakers in Formula 1, but Nunn's limited finances meant that he could not afford to employ top drivers. As an example of the will to succeed without large financial backing, Morris Nunn is an object lesson to everyone, and in 1977 his earlier efforts bore fruit with a large budget from a Swiss firm and the employment of Gianclaudio

Regazzoni to drive the new MN06 and the later MN07. For the latter half of 1977 Nunn built a further car, MN08 which was bought by Hong Kong businessman Teddy Yip for Frenchman Patrick Tambay to drive.

Year: 1976
Model: F1-N176
Engine: Cosworth DFV
Number of cylinders: 8 in-vee
Bore and Stroke: 85·6 × 64·8 mm
Capacity: 2993 cc
Valves: 4 per cylinder, two ohcs per bank
Induction: Lucas fuel-injection
Wheelbase: 8 ft 6¾ in
Forward Speeds: 5 Hewland

Front Suspension: Independent, double wishbones and coil springs
Rear Suspension: Independent, single transverse top link, twin lower links, double radius rods and coil spring
Chassis Frame: Aluminium monocoque; engine a stressed member
Maximum Speed: 175 mph

ERA England

The English Racing Automobile came into being through the efforts of Raymond Mays and Peter Berthon, who had been racing a supercharged 6-cylinder Riley in 1933. In it they could see the basis for a pure single-seater with International ability. Humphrey Cook supplied financial backing and, with Reid Railton on the chassis design and Murray Jamieson on the super-charging and the engine, the first ERA was completed in May 1934. It was a functional single-seater with a supercharged 6-cylinder 1½-litre engine and 4-speed pre-selector gearbox. Between that time and when war put a stop to racing in 1939, they completed eighteen cars at their small works at Bourne in Lincolnshire, starting with the A-type, of which four were built, then the slightly improved B-type, of which thirteen were built, with later modifications of these producing the C and D-types, and in 1939 there appeared the E-type which was an entirely new design by Berthon.

In 1935/6/7 the B-type ERAs made a reputation in International 'voiturette' racing and many of them are still racing in Historic racing car events. Perhaps the most successful in the pre-war years was R2B, the car bought for Prince Bira of Thailand, by his cousin Prince Chula. The history of this car between 1935 and 1939 was outstanding and after its last race with Bira in 1946 it was kept in Devon by Chula, later passing into the National Motor Museum. In 1976 after being completely rebuilt, it appeared in VSCC events, racing again successfully after a rest of 30 years.

By pre-war standards of GP car the ERA was not a front-line racing car, but it was well able to stand alongside contemporary 1½-litre cars of the time. It had inherent reliability and this produced victories against more advanced designs that were a bit temperamental. In 1939 the first E-type was built but never developed properly, for the firm changed hands and moved to Dunstable and the upheavals affected the preparation of the new car. Mays and Berthon were no longer connected with the firm, but Mays continued to race an ex-works car as a private owner. This was R4D, which was uprated from the original B-series car with C-type i.f.s. and Zoller supercharging, hydraulic braking and many chassis improvements.

After the war Mays and Berthon formed the BRM syndicate and ERA Ltd specialized in design and development work for the motor industry after completing the second E-type. Attempts were made to develop the E-types but without success, and a new car was built, using a 2-litre Bristol engine and gearbox, this being known as the G-type. It was notable for some advanced chassis and suspension design features, and the use of light alloys, but it was not successful and it was sold to the Bristol Car Division who used it as the basis for some sports/racing cars.

Of the pre-war ERAs only one was ever destroyed, the remainder all being in good health and many of them still racing in VSCC events. Even the two E-types have been reclaimed from the grave, one having been badly burnt in a crash and the other made into a sports car with a Jaguar engine.

right Marcel Lehoux in ERA R3B in the Prince Rainier Cup at Monaco in 1936

below Leslie Johnson about to test the E-type ERA GP1 on an airfield in 1949

Year: 1936
Model: B-type
Engine: ERA
Number of cylinders: 6
Bore and Stroke: 57·5 × 95·2 mm
Capacity: 1488 cc
Valves: Inclined overhead with pushrods

Induction: Jamieson-Roots supercharger
Wheelbase: 7 ft 10 in
Forward Speeds: 4 ENV preselector
Front and Rear Suspension: Semi-elliptic leaf springs
Chassis Frame: Channel-section
Maximum Speed: 130 mph

Year: 1939
Model: E-type
Engine: ERA
Number of cylinders: 6
Bore and Stroke: 62·8 × 80 mm
Capacity: 1488 cc
Valves: Inclined overhead with pushrods
Induction: Zoller supercharger

Wheelbase: 8 ft 7 in
Forward Speeds: 4
Front Suspension: Independent by trailing arms and torsion bars
Rear Suspension: de Dion with torsion bars
Chassis Frame: Tubular
Maximum Speed: 150 mph

ERA-Delage   Anglo–French

Taking the 1927 Delage chassis to which Prince Chula had fitted i.f.s. just pre-war, Rob Walker installed the E-type ERA engine from GP1, the first of the E-types which was crashed and burnt in the Isle of Man. An Armstrong-Siddeley pre-selector gearbox was used, and the offset driving position and the external appearance of the car was kept original, including the square Delage radiator shell. Modern brakes, shock-absorbers, wheels and tyres were fitted and the car was raced by Tony Rolt. It proved to be a most

Tony Rolt watches the ERA-Delage being worked on at a Boreham Airfield race meeting in 1951

successful combination and enlivened the 1951/2 seasons on the British circuits, one of its best performances being a 3rd place at Goodwood, behind a Tipo 159 Alfa Romeo and a 4½-litre Ferrari.

The 1½-litre 6-cylinder E-type ERA engine was fitted with a two-stage supercharging system, with two Roots blowers, one in front of the engine and the other alongside the engine. Owned for a long time by a member of the VSCC and raced in Historic events, it was kept in superb condition.

Year: 1927/51
Model: Grand Prix
Engine: ERA
Number of cylinders: 6
Bore and Stroke: 62·8 × 80 mm
Capacity: 1488 cc
Valves: Inclined overhead with pushrods
Induction: Two-stage Roots supercharging

Wheelbase: 8 ft 2½ in
Forward Speeds: 4 pre-selector
Front Suspension: Independent by transverse leaf spring and upper wishbones
Rear Suspension: Rigid axle on semi-elliptic leaf springs
Chassis Frame: Channel-section
Maximum Speed: 140 mph

Ferguson   England

The firm started in 1939 by F.W. Dixon and A.P.R. Rolt, to do research on 4-w-d was supported after the war by Harry Ferguson the tractor 'king' and known as Harry Ferguson Research Ltd. Prototype car-building gradually led to building a Formula 1 car. This was done in 1961 and in less than twelve months from the first drawings the Ferguson 4-w-d racing car won the Oulton Park Gold Cup race, only the third event in which it had competed. The design team of Ferguson Research was led by Claude Hill and Tony Rolt,

Stirling Moss in the Ferguson P99 during practice for the Oulton Park Cup which he won

and the car, known as Project 99, broke new ground apart from its 4-w-d. The layout of its wishbone suspension provided more rigidity for less weight, and the inboard mounting of the four disc brakes was an improvement over previous attempts at this means of saving unsprung weight. It incorporated a Dunlop 'Maxaret' anti-locking device in its braking system—a mechanism used for many years on aircraft.

At a time when GP contestants were building their cars with engines mounted behind the driver, the Ferguson had its 4-cylinder Coventry-Climax engine mounted in front. With 4-w-d it is more advantageous to have equal weight distribution on all wheels, rather than the bias to the rear, desirable with a 2-wheel-drive car. There had been many 4-w-d cars before the Ferguson, but to this car must go the credit of being the first with this form of transmission to win a motor race on a road circuit. By clever detail design work, and thanks to some of the basic principles of 4-w-d, the Ferguson suffered no weight handicap in comparison with its rivals. By distributing the engine power to all four wheels, tyres of only 5·50-in section could be used, whereas rival makes used 6·50-in on the rear. Similarly drive-shafts, differentials and suspension members could all be reduced in weight, compared to orthodox designs. The Ferguson system of 4-w-d differed from previous attempts at solving the problem by the use of a third differential and slipping clutch between the front and rear axles; this eliminated the possibility of wheel spin at either end and, in consequence, there was no necessity for weighty self-locking differentials.

Designed primarily as a research vehicle, to enable Ferguson to do tests of stability, braking and so on, at high speeds, the P99 was raced where suitable to justify the claims of 4-w-d, and prove the results of years of experimental work. In 1963 it was taken to Australia and New Zealand for the Tasman races, and in 1964 was used by Peter Westbury to win the British Hill-climb Championship. It was then kept at Ferguson Research Ltd. until 1973 when the Donington Park Racing Car Museum was opened, whereupon it was loaned for permanent display and holds pride of place in the 4-wheel-drive section.

Year: 1961
Model: P99
Engine: Coventry-Climax
Number of cylinders: 4
Bore and Stroke: 81·9 × 71·1 mm
Capacity: 1498 cc
Valves: Inclined overhead with two ohcs
Induction: Two double-choke Weber carburettors

Wheelbase: 7 ft 6 in
Forward Speeds: 5 Colotti
Front and Rear Suspension:
Independent by wishbones and coil springs, incorporating driveshafts
Chassis Frame: Tubular spaceframe
Maximum Speed: 150 mph

Ferrari Italy

It is unlikely that any racing-car manufacturer has built as many different racing models as Enzo Ferrari—the only types of racing he has not supported since 1947 have been 500-cc Formula 3, and subsequent Formula 3 categories, and those forms of racing which specify the engine allowed.

A true racing-car manufacturer, who has always built his entire car, engine, gearbox and chassis, Ferrari began in earnest in 1947 with racing/sports cars, and in 1948 entered Formula 1 racing in which he has participated ever since, despite numerous setbacks. Enzo Ferrari was active in racing in the early 1920s, as a member of the Alfa Romeo team, and later took over the official Alfa Romeo racing, with his Scuderia Ferrari. In 1940 he built the first Ferrari car, a sports model based on two Fiat 1100-cc engines in line on a common crankcase, but war put a stop to this activity.

Alberto Ascari with a Tipo 125 Ferrari in the 1949 Swiss GP at Berne

Ferrari persevered with supercharged GP 1½-litre cars, with Gioacchino Colombo as chief designer, during 1948/9/50, developing from single-ohc V12 engines, with one supercharger, to twin-ohc V-12 cylinders, with two-stage supercharging, but all the time he was chasing Alfa Romeo technical development that had many years' lead on him. In 1950 he stopped super-charged development and replaced Colombo by Aurelio Lampredi, whom he set to work on a programme of 4½-litre V12-cylinder engines, unsuper-charged. By high-pressure work these cars were successful before the end of the season, and in 1951 finally defeated the Alfa Romeo team. For the Formula 2 years of 1952/3 Ferrari was to the fore, with unblown 4-cylinder cars, and these he developed into the basis for his 1954 GP cars for the new Formula 1. His close rival, Maserati, had the edge on these Ferrari cars, and, of course, Mercedes-Benz also defeated the Maranello cars. Just when things

left Wolfgang von Trips in a Tipo 246 Ferrari in the 1958 German GP at Nurburgring

right John Surtees driving a Tipo 1512 Ferrari in the 1965 German GP at the Nurburgring

looked black for Ferrari's GP hopes, the Lancia firm sold out and gave all their racing cars and equipment to the Scuderia Ferrari. Lampredi was replaced by Bellantani and Jano, and Enzo Ferrari took on a new lease of life with the Lancia V8 cars. He modified, improved, and rebuilt them and built his own version of their four ohc V8 engines, winning the Manufacturers' Award with these Lancia/Ferraris in 1956. By the end of 1957 they had reached the end of their development, but Ferrari was already off on a new course, with a V6-cylinder engine of his own design, named the Dino, after his son who had just died of illness.

The Dino 2½-litre GP Ferrari gave Mike Hawthorn his 1958 World Championship, and just missed winning the Manufacturers' Championship for Ferrari. The team went on with the development of the Dino V6 engine, both as a 2½-litre and a 1½-litre, and in 1961 Ferrari bowed to design trends and built his GP cars, now 1½ litres by the rules, with the engine behind the driver. In 1961 Ferrari was Champion Manufacturer, as well as providing the car for World Champion Driver Phil Hill. During the years of the 1½-litre Formula, Ferrari engines went from V6 to V8 and to flat-12 cylinder layouts and his chassis design kept pace with all the new innovations.

When the new 3-litre Formula was introduced in 1966 Ferrari was ready with a V12-cylinder car, using engine design and development from his sports-car racing programme. Various forms of the V12-cylinder engine kept Ferrari cars in the forefront in ensuing years, but the compact Cosworth V8-powered cars from Britain were proving more than a match for anything that came from Maranello. In 1970 a new generation of Ferrari engines appeared on the GP scene, in the form of a 12-cylinder 'boxer' motor, an horizontally opposed engine with banks of 6 cylinders on each side. By now Mauro Forghieri was in full charge of technical development. With these came the adoption of semi-monocoque construction and stressed-skin concepts using the engine as an integral part of the design. From the original Ferrari B1 all Formula 1 Ferraris have been on the flat-12 principle and the latest cars, with transverse gearbox layout ahead of the final drive, are very sophisticated cars in all respects, well able to stand comparison with any

other designs. For a long time Ferrari's main advantage over his rivals was engine design and power output, but today he has advantages of road-holding and handling over many of his rivals, as well as engine advantages.

The original Colombo-designed GP Ferrari of 1948 had a 60-degree V12-cylinder engine, with single camshaft, chain-driven, to each bank of cylinders, operating inclined valves through rockers, and this basic layout has appeared in racing Ferraris, both GP and sports cars, in 1½-litre, 2-litre, 2·3-litre, 2·7-litre, 2·9-litre, 3·3-litre, 3·5-litre, 4·0-litre, 4·1-litre, 4·5-litre and 4·9-litre forms, and even a very rare 6·9-litre for Can-Am racing. Above all else, Enzo Ferrari is an engine builder. In addition he has built 4-cylinder, in-line 6-cylinder, V6-cylinder, V8-cylinder and flat-12-cylinder engines, and even built an experimental vertical-twin engine. He has never again built a straight-8-cylinder engine, since his first in 1940.

In the early days Ferrari sold racing cars as well as running a factory team, having a special servicing section to look after the customers' GP cars, but when he took over the Lancia team he stopped building racing cars for sale, and concentrated all his efforts on the works team. Apart from one or two special cars sold to Pat Hoare in New Zealand, there have not been any racing Ferraris in private hands for a number of years. In recent years he has sold off some of his obsolete Formula 1 cars to collectors and museums, but purely as 'demonstration' vehicles. As well as supporting GP racing to the full Ferrari built a special 4·1-litre car, on GP lines, for the 1958 Monza 500 Mile Race on the banked track. This car was more than a match for the Indianapolis cars of the day, on sheer speed, but it did not ride the bankings as well, though it lapped at 175 mph. An abortive track-racing Ferrari was the Bardahl Special, built in 1956 at the instigation of Guiseppe Farina, in which a 4·1-litre 6-cylinder sports-car engine was installed in a Kurtis Kraft chassis. In 1967 Ferrari made a brief foray into Formula 2 with a V6-engined car, using the production Dino engine as a basis.

Since the merger with the great Fiat empire, who look after production and sales of road-going Ferraris, the Grand Old Man of racing has been able to spend all his time on his racing team, building racing cars for his own enjoyment and the use of his own team, without the necessity of following it up with production work; Fiat engineers do all that for him. To build racing cars for Formula 1 GP racing for nearly 30 unbroken years, and successful ones at that, is a record that few people can hope to claim or attain and today Ferrari cars are admired and respected wherever they appear.

Niki Lauda competing with a Tipo 312/T2 Ferrari in the 1977 Monaco GP

Year: 1949
Model: Tipo 125
Engine: Ferrari (front mounted)
Number of cylinders: 12 in-vee
Bore and Stroke: 55 × 52·5 mm
Capacity: 1498 cc
Valves: Inclined overhead with single camshaft to each bank
Induction: Single supercharger
Wheelbase: 7 ft 1 in

Forward Speeds: 5
Front Suspension: Independent by double wishbones and transverse leaf spring
Rear Suspension: Independent by swing axle and transverse leaf spring
Chassis Frame: Tubular
Maximum Speed: 150 mph

Year: 1951
Model: Tipo 375
Engine: Ferrari (front mounted)
Number of cylinders: 12 in-vee
Bore and Stroke: 80 × 74·5 mm
Capacity: 4498 cc
Valves: Inclined overhead with single camshaft to each bank
Induction: Three down-draught four-choke carburettors

Wheelbase: 7 ft 6 in
Forward Speeds: 4
Front Suspension: Independent by double wishbones and transverse leaf spring
Rear Suspension: de Dion with transverse leaf spring
Chassis Frame: Tubular
Maximum Speed: 180 mph

Year: 1952/3
Model: Tipo 500
Engine: Ferrari (front mounted)
Number of cylinders: 4
Bore and Stroke: 90 × 78 mm
Capacity: 1985 cc
Valves: Inclined overhead with two ohcs
Induction: Horizontal carburettors

Wheelbase: 7 ft 2½ in
Forward Speeds: 4
Front Suspension: Independent by double wishbones and transverse leaf spring
Rear Suspension: de Dion with transverse leaf spring
Chassis Frame: Tubular
Maximum Speed: 150 mph

Year: 1958
Model: Tipo 256 Dino
Engine: Ferrari (front mounted)
Number of cylinders: 6 in-vee 65-degrees
Bore and Stroke: 86 × 71 mm
Capacity: 2474 cc
Valves: Inclined overhead with four ohcs
Induction: Downdraught Weber carburettors

Wheelbase: 7 ft 3½ in
Forward Speeds: 4
Front Suspension: Independent by double wishbones and coil springs
Rear Suspension: de Dion with transverse leaf spring
Chassis Frame: Tubular
Maximum Speed: 170 mph

Year: 1963
Model: Tipo 156B
Engine: Ferrari (rear mounted)
Number of cylinders: 6 in-vee 120-degrees
Bore and Stroke: 73 × 58·8 mm
Capacity: 1476·6 cc
Valves: Inclined overhead with four ohcs
Induction: Bosch fuel-injection

Wheelbase: 7 ft 6½ in
Forward Speeds: 5
Front Suspension: Independent by double wishbones and coil springs
Rear Suspension: Independent by transverse links, radius rods and coil springs
Chassis Frame: Tubular space-frame
Maximum Speed: 160 mph

Year: 1977
Model: Tipo 312/T2
Engine: Ferrari (rear mounted)
Number of cylinders: 12 horizontally opposed
Bore and Stroke: 80 × 49·6 mm
Capacity: 2992 cc
Valves: 4 per cylinder, two ohcs per bank
Induction: Lucas fuel-injection

Wheelbase: 8 ft 4¾ in
Forward Speeds: 5
Front Suspension: Independent by lower wishbones, upper rocker arms and inboard coil springs
Chassis Frame: Aluminium monocoque; engine a stressed member
Maximum Speed: 190 mph

Fittipaldi

The Brazilian Fittipaldi brothers, Emerson and Wilson, developed the competitive urge at a very early age, encouraged by their father who had long been an 'afficionado' of GP racing. The brothers arrived in Europe to become professional racing drivers and both progressed into Formula 1, Emerson proving to be the best of the two, joining Team Lotus and winning the World Championship in 1972. Wilson spent a season with the Brabham team in 1973 and then returned to Brazil to start a very ambitious project, that of building a Brazilian Formula 1 car. He bought a number of British Formula 1 cars just as they became obsolete, for study purposes and with his friend Richard Divila he built the first Fittipaldi car with finance from the Brazilian Copersucar firm. It was completed in time for the opening of the 1975 season but though it was fabricated in Brazil, it was really nothing more than a British 'kit-car' built around the inevitable Cosworth DFV engine and Hewland gearbox.

The project suffered a major setback in its first race, in Argentina, when the rear suspension broke and FD/01 spun into the guard rail and caught fire. Wilson Fittipaldi was unhurt, and a second car was made ready in time for their home GP. When they started the European season they set up an English base in Reading, Berkshire and took part in most of the Championship meetings with FD/02 and FD/03, but made little progress from the back of the field.

A new car was designed for 1976 and with little warning Emerson announced that he was leaving the McLaren team, for whom he had won the World Championship in 1974, and was going to drive for his brother. Much was expected of this combination, and it started well in the Brazilian GP but then made little progress at all. A freelance designer was employed to help sort out the problems of handling and suspension, but there was no visible improvement. They tried to run a two-car team, with the young Brazilian

left The 1976 Fittipaldi car FD/04 at its Press showing in Brazil, the racing team being financed by the Brazilian Copersucar firm

right The very smooth Miller-Ford V8 built for the 1935 Indianapolis 500 Mile race, with its production-type radiator grille and V8 insignia on the side

Ingo Hoffmann in a second car, but had to abandon the idea as they could never get Emerson's car going satisfactorily, let alone a second car, though they built a total of four cars in the FD/04 series, before progressing to the FD/05. The F5 series of 1978 proved the most successful.

Year: 1976	*Forward Speeds:* 5 Hewland
Model: FD/04	*Front Suspension:* Independent by
Engine: Cosworth DFV	double wishbones and coil springs
Number of cylinders: 8 in-vee	*Rear Suspension:* Independent by
Bore and Stroke: 85·6 × 64·8 mm	single transverse top link, twin lower
Capacity: 2993 cc	links, radius rods and coil springs
Valves: 4 per cylinder, two ohcs	*Chassis Frame:* Aluminium
per bank	monocoque; engine a stressed
Induction: Lucas fuel-injection	member
Wheelbase: 7 ft 11¾ in	*Maximum Speed:* 175 mph

Ford America

Henry Ford built some special racing machines at the turn of the century, his famous '999' being capable of 90 mph, but, generally speaking, Ford, like so many big manufacturers, eschewed motor racing. In 1935 the Ford factory relented slightly and made some special racing V8-cylinder engines which were delivered to Harry Miller to build into fwd cars for Indianapolis, on the proviso that no Ford publicity should be connected with them. Later this was withdrawn and the cars were emblazoned with the V8 insignia and had radiator shells like the current production V8 cars. They were very sleek and smooth, but were not successful so the Ford Company quickly lost interest.

In the 1960s Ford took a big interest in motor racing, challenging all-comers in long-distance sports-car racing with factory Ford V8 cars. This onslaught

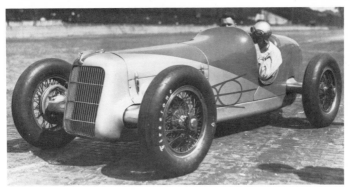

on the sport also included producing racing engines for Indianapolis, to be used in Lotus cars. The first was a racing version of the production pushrod ohv engine, but this led to a pure racing engine with 4 ohc that dominated the Indianapolis and USAC scene in 4·2-litre form, and later in turbo-charged 2·6-litre form. Although supplying engines and finance for the Lotus Indy cars, Ford did not produce a complete car for this form of racing.

Year: 1935
Model: Indianapolis Miller-Ford
Engine: Ford
Number of cylinders: 8 in-vee
Bore and Stroke: 77·79 × 95·25 mm
Capacity: 3622 cc
Valves: Side-by-side
Induction: Carburettors
Wheelbase: 8 ft 6 in

Forward Speeds: 3
Front Suspension: Independent with fwd and transverse quarter-elliptic leaf springs
Rear Suspension: Independent as front
Chassis Frame: Channel-section
Maximum Speed: 125 mph

Frazer Nash   England

Archie Frazer-Nash was the 'N' of GN and when he left that firm he began building cars under his own name. They started as GNs and at first there was some confusion and argument over racing successes with V-twin Frazer Nash cars that were really GNs. Manufacture of sports cars with 4-cylinder engines followed, still keeping the GN type of transmission by chains and dogs, there being a chain for each speed, whether three or four. Many Frazer Nash sports cars were run stripped of road equipment in racing categories and made a good name in amateur 1½-litre racing in the Vintage years. The firm was taken over by the Aldington brothers in the late '20s, who continued a strong racing activity, always with 'production' machines.

The Frazer Nash chassis was simple and ideally suited to conversion into a single-seater special. Many cars were built by amateur enthusiasts, though it was not until 1935 that Frazer Nash Cars offered a single-seater for sale. This was fitted with a twin-supercharged Albert Gough-designed ohc 1½-litre engine, improved front axle and brakes and duplex chains for the transmission of its 150 bhp. Only three of these single-seaters were built and they were more at home in sprints and hill-climbs than in full-length races. The factory ran a single-seater for A.F.P. Fane and with it he broke the Shelsley Walsh record in 1937. This car now resides in the Donington Park Racing Car Museum, slightly modified over the years, but another car in almost original form exists in private hands and used to be seen in VSCC events.

When Frazer Nash cars became Bristols after the war, an attempt was made to join in Formula 2 racing. This began in 1952 with a fairly conventional car, using production Frazer Nash/Bristol parts. It was a single-seater with front-mounted Bristol engine and gearbox, standard i.f.s. and rigid back axle. As it was trying to beat the successful Cooper-Bristol of those days its task was pretty hopeless and it did not get very far.

A.F.P. Fane in the supercharged single-seater Frazer Nash during his record-breaking run at Shelsley Walsh in 1937

Year: 1935
Model: Single-seater
Engine: Gough
Number of cylinders: 4
Bore and Stroke: 69 × 100 mm
Capacity: 1496 cc
Valves: In-line overhead with single ohc
Induction: Two Centric superchargers

Wheelbase: 9 ft 0 in
Forward Speeds: 4 chains
Front Suspension: Straight beam on cantilevered half-elliptic springs
Rear Suspension: Quarter elliptic leaf springs
Chassis Frame: Channel-section
Maximum Speed: 125 mph

Ken Wharton driving the factory Bristol-engined Frazer Nash in the 1952 Swiss GP on the Bremgarten circuit

Year: 1952
Model: Formula 2
Engine: Bristol
Number of cylinders: 6
Bore and Stroke: 66 × 96 mm
Capacity: 1971 cc
Valves: Inclined overhead with cross-pushrods
Induction: Three down-draught carburettors

Wheelbase: 8 ft 0 in
Forward Speeds: 4
Front Suspension: Independent by wishbones and transverse leaf spring
Rear Suspension: Rigid axle on torsion bars
Chassis Frame: Tubular
Maximum Speed: 135 mph

Freikaiserwagen
England

The Dr. Porsche designed Auto Union of the mid-30s inspired the cousins David and Joe Fry with Dick Caesar to build a sprint-car modelled on the lines of the P-Wagen, hence the name Freikaiserwagen. They used a chain-driven GN chassis, Morgan 3-wheeler front suspension, and a supercharged V-twin Blackburne air-cooled engine mounted transversely in the frame behind the driver, while the fuel tank, taken from a light aeroplane, was of aerofoil section and supported on struts above the engine. Driven by Joe Fry, this rare vehicle was a remarkable performer. In 1948 it underwent vast development with the aid of R.R. Jackson. The Blackburne engine was strengthened and two-stage supercharging was fitted, the two Marshall blowers delivering at 14 lb/in^2. The unit was turned through 90 degrees so that it was in line with the chassis, which was now tubular, and chain drive went to a Norton motor-cycle gearbox, then to a layshaft and finally down to a central sprocket on the rear axle incorporating a ZF differential. The

Joe Fry leaving the Esses at the Prescott hill-climb in 1949 with the Freikaiserwagen in its ultimate form. The badge on the front simply reads FRY

same front suspension was retained, but the rear suspension was made independent by swing axles with free-mounted rubber strands in tension.

In this form, using special alcohol fuel and a 48-mm SU carburettor, some 120 bhp was developed and it was one of the most potent sprint cars in existence. Joe Fry took the Shelsley Walsh record with it in 1949. Unfortunately he overdid it at a hill-climb at Blandford and killed himself in 1950, and cousin David put the wreckage away and never rebuilt it.

Year: 1937
Model: Special
Engine: Blackburne
Number of cylinders: V-twin
Bore and Stroke: 85 × 96·8 mm
Capacity: 1097 cc
Valves: Inclined overhead with pushrods
Induction: Single Marshall supercharger

Wheelbase: 7 ft 3 in
Forward Speeds: 4 chains
Front Suspension: Morgan vertical sliding pillars with coil springs
Rear Suspension: Quarter-elliptic leaf springs and radius plates to GN beam
Chassis Frame: Channel-section
Maximum Speed: 100 mph

Year: 1948
Model: Special
Engine: Blackburne (Jackson)
Number of cylinders: V-twin
Bore and Stroke: 85 × 96·8 mm
Capacity: 1097 cc
Valves: Inclined overhead with pushrods
Induction: Two-stage Marshall supercharging

Wheelbase: 7 ft 3 in
Forward Speeds: 4 Norton gearbox
Front Suspension: Morgan vertical sliding pillars with coil springs
Rear Suspension: Swing axles with rubber in tension
Chassis Frame: Tubular 'Iota'
Maximum Speed: 110 mph

Fuzzi England

This little sprint vehicle showed, for those who were prepared to see, the advantages of 4-wheel-drive for acceleration purposes. The designer, Robert Waddy, set about building this vehicle in 1935, planning his chassis on the lines of an Avro Avian aircraft fuselage, using 18 swg chrome-molybdenum tubing, hence the name Fuzzi. It was one of the earliest examples of the space-frame. Into this he put two single-cylinder dirt-track JAP engines, one in front and one in the rear, each driving a pair of wheels through its own Rudge motorcycle gearbox by chains. With such a design, independent suspension to all four wheels was natural, and this was achieved by means of trailing arms and torsion bars at the front, and by a transverse leaf spring and a system of links resembling wishbones at the rear.

The engines were not coupled together, but the two throttles were joined to a single rocking pedal. Depressing the pedal opened both throttles, while the toe opened one and the heel the other independently, thus affording control of both engines separately to avoid unnecessary wheel spin at either end. This unusual car was a regular competitor in sprint events during the years 1936–39, the only major change being the substitution of Morgan 3-wheeler gearboxes in place of the Rudges. A time of 25·80 seconds for the standing half-mile with only 1000 cc, unblown, and 44·08 seconds up Shelsley Walsh in 1937 showed the possibilities of 4-wheel-drive.

In 1946 Robert Waddy had the idea of further developing the concept, using one large engine in place of the two small ones. Unfortunately his enthusiasm ran away with him and instead of starting from scratch he cut Fuzzi in half, lengthened it and tried to carry on from there. A Mercury V8 engine was put in the centre and a complex system of chains and shafts took the drive to the front and rear axles. With the extra power, suspension and driving members had to be redesigned until little of the original car was left apart from the conception of space-frame and 4-wheel-drive.

Poor little Fuzzi no longer existed, and in its place was a complicated contraption that defeated itself by its complexity, which due to various differences of opinion never reached fruition.

Year: 1935/9
Model: Sprint Special
Engines: JAP (two)
Number of cylinders: 1 each
Bore and Stroke: 81 × 96·8 mm
Capacity: 498 cc each
Valves: Inclined overhead with pushrods
Induction: Carburettors

Wheelbase: 5 ft 9 in
Forward Speeds: 3
Front Suspension: Independent by trailing arms and torsion bars
Rear Suspension: Independent by transverse leaf spring and links
Chassis Frame: Tubular space-frame
Maximum Speed: 100 mph

left Robert Waddy in the twin-engined, 4-wheel-drive Fuzzi at Lewes speed trials in 1936

right Keith Greene driving the 1962 Gilby powered by a V8 BRM 1½-litre engine

Gilby   England

The Gilby Engineering Company of North London was owned by Syd Greene, who was a long-time racing enthusiast, taking part in various minor competitions himself, and he formed a racing department running Maserati sports and GP cars for many years, employing professional drivers. When his son Keith became old enough to race he naturally drove the Gilby Engineering cars, which included Lotus and Cooper models. Having good engineering facilities available Syd Greene turned his attention to building his own car, on lines already set by Lotus and Cooper, and beginning with a small sports car, his designer, Len Terry, progressed to a single-seater racing car in 1960, using a 1½-litre Coventry-Climax engine and Colotti gearbox. The design did not break away from accepted principles, having all independent suspension by wishbones and coil springs, tubular space frame and rear-mounted engine, but it was built to Gilby specifications and it gave the Greene family more fun to be able to race a car of their own construction.

In 1962 they built a second Gilby car with a V8 BRM engine and 6-speed gearbox, and took part in numerous Formula 1 events, gaining some good 3rd and 4th positions behind the factory cars of the time.

Year: 1960
Model: Formula 2
Engine: Coventry-Climax
Bore and Stroke: 81·9 × 71·1 mm
Capacity: 1498 cc
Valves: Inclined overhead with two ohcs
Induction: Two double-choke Weber carburettors
Wheelbase: 7 ft 5 in

Forward Speeds: 5—Colotti
Front Suspension: Independent by wishbones, radius rods and coil springs
Rear Suspension: Independent by lower wishbone, radius rods, transverse link and coil springs
Chassis Frame: Tubular space-type
Maximum Speed: 145 mph

Goldenrod America

Constructed by California hot-rodders Bill and Bob Summers and driven by Bob Summers the 4-engined record car 'Goldenrod' took the Land Speed Record for wheel-driven cars at 409·695 mph for the kilometre and 409·277 mph for the mile in November 1965. The four Chrysler V8 engines were mounted in line driving the front and rear wheels from a shaft along the left-hand side of the car, through 4-speed gearboxes fore and aft. Tuned to over 600 bhp each, the Chrysler engines were fuel-injected and used special fuel. The driver sat behind the rear wheels in 'slingshot' dragster style, the enclosed cockpit blending neatly into a tail fin containing a braking parachute. The car was only 28 in high with a very small frontal area and was 32 ft long; it was one of the smoothest looking record cars ever seen on the Bonneville Salt Flats, with a drag co-efficient of only 0·117.

The sleek, streamlined 'Goldenrod' at Bonneville in 1965

Year: 1965
Model: Goldenrod
Engines: Chrysler 'hemi-head'
Number of cylinders: 8 in vee × 4 = 32
Bore and Stroke:
Capacity: 6·98 lites × 4 = 27·6 litres
Valves: Pushrod overhead
Induction: Fuel injection

Wheelbase: 17 ft 3 in
Forward Speeds: 4
Front Suspension: Wishbones and coil springs
Rear Suspension: None
Chassis Frame: Box-section
Maximum Speed: 415 mph

Gordini France

Amédée Gordini was active in pre-war sports-car racing with tuned French Fiats, known as Simcas. In 1947 he built single-seater cars around 1100 Simca-Fiat parts, using the pushrod 4-cylinder engine and gearbox, the front suspension and the rear axle. His engines developed 65 bhp and in the light Gordini chassis this gave a fair performance. The team ran in 'voiturette' races and had as drivers, Raymond Sommer, Jean-Pierre Wimille and Prince Bira. For the 1948 Formula 2 he built new cars, with engines enlarged to 1430 cc and having special inclined-valve cylinder heads, later enlarging these engines to 1490 cc and developing 115 bhp. In spite of giving away 500 cc to his rivals, the easy handling and light weight of the Simca-Gordinis made them very formidable on twisty circuits. It was in one of these cars that Fangio made his first racing appearance in Europe. In 1950 Gordini fitted superchargers to his 1½-litre cars and took part in full GP racing, running his Equipe in both Formula 1 and Formula 2, though in supercharged form they were not fast enough to achieve success.

For 1951 Gordini built entirely new 1490-cc engines; these 4-cylinders had two ohcs operating inclined valves through short rockers. The front suspension was still on Simca lines, with a lower wishbone and single top arm, operating a coil spring immersed in an oil bath. For 1952 he built cars that

left Maurice Trintignant in a 6-cylinder 2-litre Gordini during the 1953 Pau GP
right An 8-cylinder 2½-litre Gordini seen in the Goodwood paddock for the Easter meeting 1956

were entirely Gordini, dropping the name Simca and at the same time severing his connections with the Simca concern. The new cars had 6-cylinder 2-litre engines, with the same system of twin ohcs as his earlier engines, and the front suspension was by two transverse arms on each side, the lower one coupled to a torsion bar. The rigid rear axle was also sprung on torsion bars. These cars were very tractable, and Jean Behra drove one on the road from Paris to Switzerland when time was short before the Swiss GP. They were a great success, Behra beating all the Italians on the fast Reims circuit in the 1952 Reims GP. Unfortunately these advances cost money, and Gordini began to get into financial difficulties. The 1953 season saw the Gordini team living a hand-to-mouth existence, which deteriorated into a shambles. He tried to resurrect the Equipe for the new 1954 Formula by enlarging the

6-cylinder engines to $2\frac{1}{2}$ litres, but by now the cars were too fast for their road-holding, the rigid rear axle being the limiting factor.

Gordini was trying to complete an entirely new design, and could spare neither time nor money for the old 6-cylinder cars, so they were patched up as well as possible. The new car appeared at the end of 1955. It was an 8-cylinder-in-line two-ohcs, with independent suspension to all four wheels by a Watt-linkage system and torsion bars, but the engine did not develop sufficient power to challenge other makes. These new cars were large and heavy in comparison with the earlier Gordinis, and the whole design had departed in the wrong direction from normal Gordini principles. They struggled on through 1956 without success, and in 1957 quietly faded from the GP scene, Gordini turning his attention to experimental work for the Regie Renault concern. Eventually all the factory cars and equipment were passed to Fritz Schlumpf for his museum at Mulhouse.

Year: 1952/53
Model: Formula 2
Engine: Gordini
Number of cylinders: 6
Bore and Stroke: 75 × 75 mm
Capacity: 1986 cc
Valves: Inclined overhead with two ohcs and rockers
Induction: Three double-choke Weber carburettors

Wheelbase: 7 ft $4\frac{5}{8}$ in
Forward Speeds: 4
Front Suspension: Independent by transverse arms and torsion bars
Rear Suspension: Rigid axle on torsion bars
Chassis Frame: Tubular
Maximum Speed: 145 mph

Year: 1955/57
Model: Formula 1
Engine: Gordini
Number of cylinders: 8 in-line
Bore and Stroke: 75 × 70 mm
Capacity: 2475 cc
Valves: Inclined overhead with two ohcs and rockers
Induction: Four double-choke Weber carburettors

Wheelbase: 7 ft $4\frac{5}{8}$ in
Forward Speeds: 5
Front and Rear Suspension: Independent by Watt-link mechanism and torsion bars
Chassis Frame: Tubular
Maximum Speed: 155 mph

Hesketh   England

A short life and a gay one sums up the Hesketh Formula 1 team. Lord Hesketh decided to go motor racing in the Grand Manner and set up a small team in 1972 running a Formula 3 car to start with. Then he purchased a 1973 March

731 and designer Harvey Postlethwaite, who had been with March Engineering previously, modified it and with James Hunt driving, it proved quite competitive. In 1974 they progressed to making their own car with Cosworth DFV engine and Hewland gearbox, the Hesketh Motor Company being formed and housed in the stables of the family home at Easton Neston. This was the Type 308, quite simply 3-litre 8-cylinder. Three cars were built for Hunt's use and he achieved victory in the International Trophy at Silverstone in 1974 and in the Dutch GP in 1975. While the 308 was very much a development of the March 731 theme, their next effort was completely new. This was the 308C which was very low and squat and started the new trend for engine air-intakes designed into the bodywork rather than stuck on as an after thought. Mechanically the suspension followed conventional layout, but the springing medium was rubber in compression, after experiments had been made on the 308 cars. At the end of 1975, just as the new car was beginning to show promise, his Lordship called a halt to the racing programme.

James Hunt driving Lord Hesketh's Type 308 Formula 1 car in the French GP in 1975, carrying the patriotic red, white and blue stripes across the white car

Racing had been carried out on a rather ostentatious scale, with exotic support cars, lavish parties, helicopters, boats and all the paraphernalia of a rich young man playing at motor racing. With no end-product in sight, or purpose behind the activity it could not hope to last. The team was disbanded and Anthony Horsley who had been team-manager ran the 308 cars on a hire-deal with various amateur drivers, while the new and unfulfilled 308C was sold to the Walter Wolf/Frank Williams team and became the prototype of the Williams FW05 cars built in 1976, with designer Postlethwaite moving with the car.

Horsley kept the Hesketh Motor Company going throughout 1976 and 1977 by running a Rent-a-Drive scheme with the Type 308 cars modified to D-specification and followed these with the 308E, designed by Frank Dernie.

Year: 1977
Model: 308E
Engine: Cosworth DFV
Number of cylinders: 8 in-vee
Bore and Stroke: 85·6 × 64·8 mm
Capacity: 2993 cc
Valves: 4 per cylinder. Two ohcs
per bank
Induction: Lucas fuel-injection
Wheelbase: 8 ft 9 in
Forward Speeds: 5 Hewland

Front Suspension: Independent by
double wishbones and coil springs
Rear Suspension: Independent,
single transverse top link, twin
lower links, double radius rods and
coil springs
Chassis Frame: Aluminium
monocoque; engine a stressed
member
Maximum Speed: 180 mph

Hill
England

In his later years as a top-flight driver Graham Hill was loath to give up motor racing, for whether he was first or last he enjoyed driving a racing car. By 1973 he could no longer justify a drive in a works or professional team, so he started an organization to run a car expressly for himself. This was done with financial backing from W.D. & H.O. Wills through their Embassy Cigarette brand. He purchased the parts for a Shadow DN1 and assembled it in his own workshop, which taught him and his mechanics a great deal about chassis and suspension design and construction. The engine was no problem as the ubiquitous Cosworth-Ford DFV was used, and with a Hewland gearbox the transmission problems were solved.

After a season with this Shadow-Cosworth, Hill arranged for Lola cars to supply the fundamentals of their F5000 design so that the Hill team could construct F1 cars using the Cosworth/Hewland package. By the end of 1974 they were almost self-contained as regards the chassis, and for 1975 they incorporated so many of their own modifications to the Lola T370 that it was now the T371 and they felt justified in renaming it the GH1. During the season they constructed three more cars and the Hill Formula 1 car was truly launched.

Graham Hill gave Tony Brise a chance to drive and was so impressed with the young man's potential ability that he promptly retired from driving and concentrated on running the team. By the end of the year they had designed and built an entirely new car, the GH2 ready for the 1976 season. In November of 1975 tragedy struck. Graham was returning from a testing session at Paul Ricard, in the South of France, in his own private aircraft, with Brise, the team-manager, the designer and two mechanics on board when he crashed near Elstree Aerodrome and all six were killed. In a stroke the team had been wiped out and Embassy Racing closed down; the unraced GH2 car was put in the National Motor Museum, a fitting tribute to one of the great men in the annals of motor-racing history.

Tony Brise in the Hill GH1 during the French GP at the Paul Ricard circuit in 1975

Year: 1975
Model: GH1
Engine: Cosworth DFV
Number of cylinders: 8 in-vee
Bore and Stroke: 85·6 × 64·8 mm
Capacity: 2993 cc
Valves: 4 per cylinder, two ohcs per bank
Induction: Lucas fuel-injection
Wheelbase: 8 ft 5 in
Forward Speeds: 5 Hewland FGA 400

Front Suspension: Independent by double wishbones and coil springs
Rear Suspension: Independent, single transverse top link, twin lower links, double radius rods and coil springs.
Chassis Frame: Aluminium monocoque; engine a stressed member.
Maximum Speed: 175 mph

Honda   Japan

The Honda Motor Company of Tokyo completely dominated motorcycle racing in Europe and in 1964 set about doing the same in motor racing. They entered Formula 1 with a revolutionary 1½-litre car with a V12 engine mounted transversely amidships, running at the very high speed of 12,500 rpm. The initial entry at the Nurburgring was discreet, with an American driver with no GP experience, but the following year they took a bigger bite at the cherry, with Richie Ginther joining the team and they ended the season, and span of the 1½-litre Formula, with a win in the Mexican GP.

Concurrently, they supplied 4-cylinder 1-litre engines to Jack Brabham for use in his own chassis for Formula 2 in 1965. In 1966, he and Denis Hulme dominated the F2 scene with these Brabham-Hondas. With the introduction of the new 3-litre Formula in 1966 Honda arrived with a formidable weapon in the shape of a 90-degree V12 engine, giving 400 bhp at 10,500 rpm mounted

above Ritchie Ginther on test with the Honda RA-272 at Zandvoort in 1965
below John Surtees driving the 3-litre V12 Honda at the Nurburgring in 1968
when tall rear aerofoils were allowed

conventionally fore-and-aft behind the driver. This engine was an all-roller-bearing unit, undoubtedly powerful, but very long and very heavy. John Surtees persevered with this large Formula 1 car throughout 1967 and 1968, the power being increased to 450 bhp at nearly 12,000 rpm but the new British cars were much in advance of the Japanese, being smaller and lighter cars, albeit with less horsepower. The Honda technicians had conquered motorcycle racing and F2 by reason of superior horsepower output to their rivals, but this did not work out in Formula 1 as the size and weight over-rode any such advantage. In his attempts to guide the Japanese along the right lines John Surtees got Eric Broadley of Lola Cars to design a monocoque chassis and suspension to take the giant V12 engine, and with this 'Hondola' or 'Lolonda' he won an epic battle with Jack Brabham to win the Italian GP in 1967.

Realizing that their design concepts had gone in the wrong direction Honda began again and produced a very interesting new car in the middle of 1968. This had a 120-degree V8 air-cooled engine slung beneath a mono-coque backbone that extended rearwards from the cockpit monocoque. Everything about the car was new and lighter and the weight was right down to the 500-kg limit. There was some internal friction in the team between Surtees and the engineers over the first appearance of this new car in the 1968 French GP and while he stayed with the water-cooled V12, Jo Schlesser drove the new car. The recriminations ended in disaster when Schlesser crashed on the opening lap and was killed, the car being destroyed by fire.

At the end of the season a second air-cooled V8 car was built and appeared on test at Monza before the Italian GP, driven by David Hobbs, but it did not race. All was not well within the team and after four years of trying to dominate Formula 1 as they had dominated motorcycle racing, and failing lamentably, Sochiro Honda withdrew his team from all forms of racing and the intriguing cars from the Far East were not seen again.

Year: 1965
Model: RA 272
Engine: Honda
Number of cylinders: 12 in-vee
Bore and Stroke: 58·1 × 47 mm
Capacity: 1495 cc
Valves: 4 per cylinder. 4 ohcs
Induction: Fuel injection
Wheelbase: 7 ft 6½ in
Forward Speeds: 6

Front Suspension: Upper rocker-arm operating inboard coil spring, lower transverse link and radius rod
Rear Suspension: Single top link, lower wishbone and double radius rods, coil springs
Chassis Frame: Aluminium monocoque and tubular engine cradle
Maximum Speed: 150 mph

Year: 1967
Model: RA 300
Engine: Honda
Number of cylinders: 12 in-vee
Bore and Stroke: 78 × 52·2 mm
Capacity: 2992 cc
Valves: 4 per cylinder. 4 ohcs
Induction: Fuel injection
Wheelbase: 7 ft 10¾ in
Forward Speeds: 5

Front Suspension: Upper rocker-arm operating inboard coil spring, lower wishbone
Rear Suspension: Single top link, lower wishbone, radius rods, coil spring
Chassis Frame: Aluminium full-length monocoque
Maximum Speed: 175 mph

Year: 1968
Model: RA 302
Engine: Honda (air-cooled)
Number of cylinders: 8 in-vee 120-degrees
Bore and Stroke: 88 × 61·4 mm
Capacity: 2987·5 cc
Valves: 4 per cylinder. 4 ohcs
Induction: Fuel injection
Wheelbase: 7 ft 9 in

Forward Speeds: 5
Front Suspension: Upper rocker-arm operating inboard coil spring, lower wishbone
Rear Suspension: Single top link, lower wishbone, radius rods, coil spring
Chassis Frame: Aluminium monocoque
Maximum Speed: 175 mph

Hotchkiss   France

In the Vintage years Hotchkiss established themselves as manufacturers of good-quality cars, and in the '30s built a very beautiful 1990-cc streamlined single-seater, for record-breaking purposes. Captain Eyston and Bert Denly took the 500-mile record at 112·9 mph with this car on the Montlhéry track, and Albert Divo brought it to Brooklands for the 500 Mile Race in 1935, lapping at 110 mph and finishing 6th.

Albert Divo driving the single-seater Hotchkiss in the 500 Mile Race at Brooklands in 1935,

Year: 1935
Model: Record car
Engine: Hotchkiss
Number of cylinders: 4
Bore and Stroke: 80 × 99 mm
Capacity: 1990 cc
Valves: Pushrod ohv
Induction: Two carburettors

Wheelbase:
Forward Speeds: 4
Front Suspension: Semi-elliptic leaf springs
Rear Suspension: Semi-elliptic leaf springs
Chassis Frame: Channel-section
Maximum Speed: 125 mph

HRG   England

Formed in 1935 by Halford, Robins and Godfrey, the HRG Company produced hand-built sports cars until 1939, and carried on with the same basic car after the war, the later models using single-ohc Singer engines and gearboxes. With the advent of the simple Formula 2 rules in 1948 (2-litres unsupercharged), and the success of various sports cars made into Formula 2 cars, Peter Clark, an HRG enthusiast of long standing, decided to join in. He built a single-seater HRG, using a modified 2-litre Standard Vanguard engine and gearbox, in a shortened sports-car chassis with central seat and steering arrangements.

However, the pre-war design of chassis with rigid axles back and front and hard suspension was outclassed, and the Vanguard engine did not respond to tuning as expected. The project was dropped after one short season in 1949.

Jack Scott driving the Standard Vanguard engined HRG at Goodwood in 1949

Year: 1949
Model: F2
Engine: Standard Vanguard
Number of cylinders: 4
Bore and Stroke: 83 × 92 mm
Capacity: 1998 cc
Valves: Overhead in-line with pushrods
Induction: Carburettors

Wheelbase: 8 ft 0½ in
Forward Speeds: 3
Front Suspension: Quarter-elliptic leaf springs
Rear Suspension: Semi-elliptic leaf springs
Chassis Frame: Channel-section
Maximum Speed: 110 mph

HWM England

Taken from the initials of Hersham & Walton Motors, where the cars were built, the HWM made a name in European racing during the early 1950s. The product of John Heath and George Abecassis, the make started with a modified 2-litre Alta sports car in 1948. The following year they built a new car, using the 83·5 × 90-mm Alta engine, and ENV gearbox with a tubular chassis. Being a 2-seater, it was able to run as a sports car or, stripped of road equipment, as a Formula 2 car. After a successful season with this H.W. Alta, Heath built a team of cars for the 1950 season. These were more or less the same, but had i.r.s., and he dropped the Alta from the name, although still using the 4-cylinder Alta engine. This team had a very successful season, being the first serious post-war attempt by the English to break into the Continental monopoly of racing, and to Heath must go the credit for paving the way for the ultimate championships gained by British cars. The 1950 HWM gave Stirling Moss his entry into serious European racing and the team 'toured' Europe, making motor racing pay its way.

For 1951 single-seater cars were built to an entirely new design, having tubular chassis frames with i.f.s. by modified MG components and a de Dion rear-axle layout, sprung on quarter-elliptic springs. The engine was still the 4-cylinder 2-litre Alta, and this team of nice-looking green cars was very popular. No major changes were made for 1952, though the de Dion rear end was sprung on torsion bars, and the rear brakes were mounted inboard. Peter Collins joined them and they were still active, though not so successful as in 1951. Heath was finding that he was reaching the limit of his financial and mechanical abilities from the development point of view; his cars had only 150 bhp which could not match the Italian opposition, and for 1953 a new engine was developed. It was based on the Alta, but had a new cylinder head with gear-driven camshafts in place of the chain-driven ones. The cars were getting heavier and power output from this new engine was not sufficient to compensate for the greater weight, and the 1953 season was a bad one for HWM.

With the new Formula 1 in 1954 and no 'voiturette' racing to replace the old Formula 2, Heath had to go into the top class against big factory opposition; this was really more than he was capable of doing. He had hoped to use the promised 2½-litre V8 Coventry-Climax 'Godiva' engine in his 1954 cars, but as this engine never went into production, Heath was left high and dry. He built a 2½-litre 4-cylinder engine on the same basis as his 2-litres, but the cars were completely outclassed and faded from the racing scene. HWM branched off into sports-car racing, using Jaguar engines, and also built a *Formule Libre* single-seater, using a similar engine in a Formula 2 chassis.

After Heath was killed in a sports-car race in 1955, the HWM was finished.

Today, when racing-car building and competition is comparatively easy, it is difficult to appreciate the huge efforts that Heath made to get a team of cars into full-time racing.

Year: 1950
Model: Formula 2
Engine: Alta
Number of cylinders: 4
Bore and Stroke: 83·5 × 90 mm
Capacity: 1970 cc
Valves: Inclined overhead with two ohcs
Induction: Two double-choke Weber carburettors

Wheelbase: 7 ft 8 in
Forward Speeds: 4 ENV preselector
Front and Rear Suspension: Independent by transverse leaf spring and wishbones
Chassis Frame: Tubular
Maximum Speed: 130 mph

Year: 1952
Model: Formula 2
Engine: Alta
Number of cylinders: 4
Bore and Stroke: 83·5 × 90 mm
Capacity: 1970 cc
Valves: Inclined overhead with two ohcs
Induction: Two double-choke Weber carburettors

Wheelbase: 7 ft 9½ in
Forward Speeds: 4 ENV preselector
Front Suspension: Independent by double wishbones and coil springs
Rear Suspension: de Dion with torsion bars
Chassis Frame: Tubular
Maximum Speed: 140 mph

Invicta England

The Invicta sports car was popular at the end of the Vintage years and in the early '30s, particularly the '100-mph' model with its big 4½-litre 6-cylinder Meadows engine and low-slung chassis. This model was often raced by keen

above The streamlined Invicta before practice for the 1932 500 Mile Race
left John Heath driving an HWM in the 1952 Eifelrennen race on the Nurburgring

111

amateurs, who stripped off all the road-equipment and competed in hill-climbs, sprints and Brooklands racing, especially on the Mountain circuit. Raymond Mays and Luis Fontes were two well-known drivers who raced stripped sports cars, and similar models can still be seen in VSCC events today.

In 1931 the Invicta company built a very special single-seater from the basic sports-car components, and this car was intended for record breaking and for racing on Brooklands Outer Circuit. It used the 6-cylinder Meadows engine and a very streamlined body was built for it, even to the extent of fairings for the wheels. At the time it received much publicity as its unusual appearance attracted the popular Press photographers. Unfortunately all this publicity was wasted for Roland Hebeler crashed the car in practice for the 1932 500 Mile Race and it was completely written off.

Year: 1932
Model: Track
Engine: Meadows
Number of cylinders: 6
Bore and Stroke: 88·5 × 120·64 mm
Capacity: 4467 cc
Valves: In-line overhead with pushrods

Induction: Carburettors
Wheelbase: 9 ft 10 in
Forward Speeds: 4
Front and Rear Suspension:
Semi-elliptic leaf springs
Chassis Frame: Channel-section
Maximum Speed: Unknown

Kieft   England

When, around 1950, 500-cc racing took on serious proportions, Stirling Moss looked for something better than a Cooper, and Ray Martin, in collaboration with various specialists, produced a very advanced chassis that Moss persuaded Cyril Kieft to finance. Using a Norton engine in the rear, with swing axle rear suspension controlled by rubber strands in tension, and wishbone front suspension, the prototype Martin Kieft was one of the best Formula 3 cars ever made. The ease with which Moss would out-corner the all-conquering

left Stirling Moss in the prototype Kieft Formula 3 car with Norton engine in 1951

right The Kojima KE 007/2 during the very wet Japanese GP of 1976

Coopers was a joy to watch—he even had time to smile at the Cooper drivers as he passed them on the outside.

Cyril Kieft attempted to market replicas of the successful Moss car, but delays and inferior materials and workmanship resulted in his losing the good name that Moss had built up, and though the production Kiefts scored some successes, the Cooper regained the Formula 3 crown.

Year: 1951	*Wheelbase:* 7 ft 0 in
Model: Formula 3	*Forward Speeds:* 4
Engine: Norton	*Front Suspension:* Double wishbones
Number of cylinders: 1 air-cooled	and rubber in torsion
Bore and Stroke: 79·62 × 100 mm	*Rear Suspension:* Swing axles with
Capacity: 499 cc	rubber in tension
Valves: Inclined overhead with	*Chassis Frame:* Tubular space-
two ohcs	frame
Induction: Amal carburettor	*Maximum Speed:* 115 mph

Kojima   Japan

The Japanese moto-cross rider Matsuhisa Kojima, who has a flourishing business importing bananas to Japan, started a small engineering firm for the express purpose of building competition cars for national sports-car and small Formula racing. In 1976 Kojima Engineering started a Formula 1 project with the specific intention of competing in their own GP at the end of the season. This they achieved, though not without some high drama, for Masahiro Hasemi the driver, crashed the car during the second practice session, having already recorded a very respectable lap time. A complete new chassis was built up in the factory, not far from the Fuji Speedway, and a new car was ready by the morning of the race. In foul weather conditions this second Kojima completed the race, albeit in last place after two stops to change tyres.

Designed by Masao Ono the car was built around the British 'Kit Car' package of Cosworth-Ford DFV engine and Hewland FGA 400 gearbox/final drive unit, and followed conventional lines on suspension and general layout, though great efforts were made to keep the weight down as near the limit as possible. Finished in black the car impressed observers by its workmanlike appearance and very low build, and it was all made in Japan using as many Japanese components as possible.

Year: 1976
Model: KE 007
Engine: Cosworth DFV
Number of cylinders: 8 in-vee
Bore and Stroke: 85·6 × 64·8 mm
Capacity: 2993 cc
Valves: 4 per cylinder. Two ohcs per bank
Induction: Lucas fuel-injection
Wheelbase: 8 ft 2½ in (2500 mm)

Forward Speeds: 5
Front Suspension: Independent by double wishbones and coil springs
Rear Suspension: Independent by single top link, parallel lower links, double radius rods and coil springs
Chassis Frame: Aluminium monocoque; engine a stressed member
Maximum Speed: 180 mph

Kurtis   America

Although Indianapolis cars appeared to be built to a standard pattern in the days of the front-engined 'roadsters', there were a surprising number of variations. Frank Kurtis of California was one builder of chassis frames and axles for Indianapolis cars in the early 1950s. His 'roadster' front-engined chassis to take the 4·2-litre Meyer-Drake Offenhauser engine was popular and successful in the 500 Mile Race, but the resultant car was invariably hidden by the name of the sponsor, so that the world at large had no idea when a Kurtis chassis won the Indy 500.

Year: 1957
Model: Indy 'Roadster'
Engine: Meyer-Drake Offenhauser
Bore and Stroke 102 × 114 mm
Capacity: 4123 cc
Valves: Inclined overhead with
two ohcs
Induction: Hilborn injectors
Wheelbase: 8 ft 0 in

Forward Speed: 2
Front Suspension: Rigid axle on
torsion bars
Rear Suspension: Rigid axle on
torsion bars
Chassis Frame: Tubular space-
frame
Maximum Speed: 180 mph

Lancia

Italy

Vincenzo Lancia took part in early motor races driving a Fiat, but when he started to manufacture cars himself he stopped racing and Lancia cars did not figure in competitions. He built up a fine name for the products of his Turin firm, which remained in the Lancia family from the early part of the century until it was taken over by Fiat in 1955. Whilst Vincenzo Lancia was in control he was against racing, but after his death his son Gianni took over and immediately embarked on an ambitious racing programme. Starting with very advanced, and successful, sports cars, the Scuderia Lancia developed rapidly and Vittorio Jano designed a GP car for the 1954 Formula 1.

This first Lancia GP car, designated the D50, appeared in October 1954 and was a new concept in GP cars, containing many novel features, such as the V8-cylinder engine forming part of the space-frame chassis. The engine was mounted at an angle in the chassis so that the propellor shaft ran diagonally across the cockpit floor. Suspension was by equal-length wishbones for the front end, using a very thin transverse leaf spring, and de Dion at the rear, also with a transverse leaf spring, and with a system of interconnected telescopic shock-absorbers that did not affect roll-stiffness at the rear. The

left Bill Vukovitch in the Offenhauser-
powered Kurtis 'roadster' with which
he won the 1953 Indianapolis 500
Mile Race

right Alberto Ascari in the first D50
Lancia after initial tests on an airfield
near Turin in 1954

cars were distinctive in having long thin fuel tanks, slung on outrigger struts separate from the body, on each side.

The Lancia team started GP racing seriously in 1955 with Ascari, Villoresi and Castellotti as drivers, but their efforts were cut short in May when Ascari was killed in a sports Ferrari. This threw the team into chaos, and the next thing was that Gianni Lancia announced that the firm had gone bankrupt and had sold out to Fiat. It would seem likely that the D50 GP cars were a last final fling. All the racing cars, equipment, spares, tools, patterns, designs and so on were handed over to the Scuderia Ferrari, in the hope that they would help to uphold Italian prestige.

The cars appeared again briefly at the end of 1955 and then were absorbed into the Ferrari design plans, the name Lancia disappearing from GP racing after a short but promising life.

Year: 1955
Model: D50
Engine: Lancia
Number of cylinders: 8 in-vee
Bore and Stroke: 73·6 × 73·1 mm
Capacity: 2489 cc
Valves: Inclined overhead with two ohcs per bank
Induction: Four downdraught double-choke Solex carburettors

Wheelbase: 7 ft 6 in
Forward Speeds: 5
Front Suspension: Double wishbones and transverse leaf spring
Rear Suspension: de Dion with transverse leaf spring
Chassis Frame: Tubular space-frame with engine as stressed member
Maximum Speed: 170 mph

Lancia-Ferrari
Italy

In 1955 the Scuderia Ferrari received all the Lancia racing cars and equipment and in 1956–7 these cars formed the basis of the GP Ferraris. The cars remained basically Lancia, but were much modified by Ferrari, with different

J.M. Fangio at speed in a Lancia-Ferrari V8 during the British GP at Silverstone in 1956

bore and stroke to the engine, new chassis frames, new bodywork, different weight distribution, different suspension and brakes. Through it all the familiar bark of the Lancia V8 engine remained little changed. When Ferrari produced his V6-cylinder Dino cars, the whole team of Lancia-Ferrari cars was broken up, only some engines being retained by the Maranello firm.

Year: 1956
Model: D50
Engine: Lancia
Number of cylinders: 8 in-vee
Bore and Stroke: 76 × 68·5 mm
Capacity: 2487 cc
Valves: Inclined overhead with two ohcs per bank
Induction: Four down-draught double-choke Weber carburettors

Wheelbase: 7 ft 6 in
Forward Speeds: 5
Front Suspension: Double wishbones and coil springs
Rear Suspension: de Dion with transverse leaf spring
Chassis Frame: Tubular space-frame
Maximum Speed: 170 mph

Lec England

David Purley raced for a number of years in various categories with cars bought from specialist manufacturers but always had them maintained and prepared in his own workshops in the family refrigeration firm of Lec in Bognor Regis, Sussex. After building a March powered by a special Ford V6 racing engine virtually from scratch for *Formule Libre* racing, Purley decided to build his own Formula 1 car and employed freelance designer Mike Pilbeam to do the drawing-board work. The car could have been called a Pilbeam, but as Purley's father was helping with the finance the family trade-name of Lec was given to the car and its type number was CRP-1, the initials of Charlie Purley.

The car made its debut at Brands Hatch early in 1977 and then took part

David Purley practising for the Spanish GP in 1977 in the Lec on the Jarama circuit

in the GP season, proving to be a very reliable and sound design. David was enjoying his Formula 1 racing enormously when his progress was cut short by a monumental accident at Silverstone in practice for the British GP. It destroyed the car and the injuries that Purley received put paid to any further racing. The cause of the crash was traced to fire-extinguisher powder, used earlier in the day to quell a small petrol fire in the injection system. This had entered the throttle slides, later solidifying and causing them to jam wide open on the approach to Beckett's Corner.

Year: 1977
Model: CRP-1
Engine: Cosworth DFV
Number of cylinders: 8 in-vee
Bore and Stroke: 85·6 × 64·8 mm
Capacity: 2993 cc
Valves: 4 per cylinder, two ohcs per bank
Induction: Lucas fuel-injection
Wheelbase: 8 ft 10½ in

Forward Speed: 5 Hewland
Front Suspension: Double wishbones and coil springs
Rear Suspension: Transverse links, radius rods and coil springs
Chassis Frame: Aluminium monocoque; engine a stressed member
Maximum Speed: 175 mph

Lightweight Special   England

In 1937 Alec Issigonis designed a sprint and hill-climb car, incorporating many unusual features. It was in 1939 that the Issisgonis 'Lightweight Special' appeared, driven by his partner J.M.P. Dowson. As the name suggests everything had been done to reduce weight. The chassis frame of deep box-section was made from plywood, faced on both sides by aluminium sheet, while the suspension to all four wheels was independent. The front was by short wishbones, the top ones forming a bell-crank which compressed rubber rings within a transverse tube. At the rear a swing-axle layout was used with rubber bands stretched over the half-axles, while the wheels were of light alloy with integral brake drums. The aluminium body was 'in-one' with the chassis frame. The engine and gearbox were from one of the supercharged side-valve works Austin 7 racing cars, while the rear axle was also racing Austin 7.

In 1946 the Lightweight Special reappeared in sprints and hill-climbs, invariably winning its class throughout the next three years, shared by Dowson and Issingonis. The side-valve Austin engine was removed and in its place was installed an experimental engine from the Wolseley factory where Issigonis was working.

This was a 748-cc 4-cylinder unit with single ohc, and a large Zoller super-charger blowing at 28 lb/in². It developed 95 bhp at 7200 rpm and as the dry weight of the car was only 720 lb it had an exciting performance as a hill-climb car.

It was withdrawn from competition in 1950 when Issigonis became too busy with design work for the Nuffield Group and the BMC, and in the 1960s it re-appeared in VSCC events.

Year: 1937/50
Model: Special
Engine: Wolsley experimental
Number of cylinders: 4
Bore and Stroke: 61 × 44 mm
Capacity: 748 cc
Valves: In-line overhead with single ohc
Induction: Zoller supercharger
Wheelbase: 7 ft. 1 in
Forward Speeds: 4
Front Suspension: Independent by double wishbones and rubber in compression
Rear Suspension: Independent by swing axles and rubber in tension
Chassis Frame: Plywood and aluminium stressed-skin
Maximum Speed: 110 mph

above Alec Issigonis driving the Lightweight Special in the 1948 Luton Hoo speed trials. The pressed-steel front wheels were not the normal wear

below Jacque Laffite on test at the Paul Ricard circuit with the first of the 1977 Ligier JS7 cars

Ligier
France

After building sports/racing cars and small-production GT cars, Guy Ligier embarked on an ambitious Formula 1 programme with the backing of Gitanes Cigarettes and the Matra engine company, starting research into the design in 1974. Ligier classified all his cars after the initials of his close friend, the late Jo Schlesser, so that the new car was the JS5 series and used a Matra

V12 engine and Hewland gearbox. The whole project progressed exactly as planned and the prototype car was shown to the world in October 1975. It took part in its first race in Brazil in January 1976 and throughout the season the car became progressively more competitive. The driver was Jacques Laffite and one of the best efforts was to achieve fastest practice lap at Monza for the Italian GP. Victory evaded the Ligier JS5 during 1976, but it was very close at times, and in one short season established a strong position in Formula 1.

Fiercely proud of being a French national team, the Ligier is predominantly French blue, though the colour scheme of the car follows that of Gitanes Cigarettes (the other French cigarette!). The workmanship on the aluminium monocoque chassis, fibreglass body panels and suspension and mechanical components is to a very high standard of integrity and shows a lot of *Engins Matra* influence. Although rather large and bulky by the standards of its rivals, the Ligier lacked nothing in speed and handling and though self-contained and close the Ligier team are worthy representatives of France.

During 1976 a second car was completed to supplement JS5/01, while the mock-up prototype car was used by Gitanes for promotional purposes. By the start of 1977 a brand-new car, the JS7 was on test, to form the spearhead for the new season. It had a new design of monocoque chassis and greatly revised aerodynamic features, though the basic elements were unchanged. Three cars were built and Jacques Laffite brought the marque its first GP victory in Sweden 1977. By means of a spacer between engine and gearbox the wheelbase can be lengthened on the JS7.

Year: 1976
Model: JS5
Engine: Matra
Number of cylinders: 12 in-vee
Bore and Stroke: 79·7 × 50 mm
Capacity: 2993 cc
Valves: 4 per cylinder with two ohcs per bank
Induction: Fuel injection
Wheelbase: 8 ft 6¼ in

Forward Speeds: 5
Front Suspension: Independent by wishbones and coil springs
Rear Suspension: Single transverse top link, double bottom links, double radius rods and coil springs
Chassis Frame: Aluminium monocoque
Maximum Speed: 185 mph

Lister-Climax
England

After making successful sports cars using proprietary engines, during the 1950s, Brian Lister of Cambridge tried his hand at a Formula 2 single-seater for the new class of racing in 1957. Using a Coventry-Climax engine, Bristol gearbox and many other proprietary parts, he assembled them all into a square-tube space-frame, but whereas his sports cars had been a success, the Formula 2 car was a failure. After a few spasmodic appearances the project was abandoned.

Year: 1957
Model: Formula 2
Engine: Coventry-Climax
Number of cylinders: 4
Bore and Stroke: 81·2 × 71·1 mm
Capacity: 1475 cc
Valves: Inclined overhead with two ohcs
Induction: Horizontal carburettors
Wheelbase: 7 ft 5 in
Forward Speeds: 4
Front Suspension: Double wishbones and coil springs
Rear Suspension: de Dion, with coil springs
Chassis Frame: Tubular space-frame
Maximum Speed: 120 mph

above Brian Lister with the tiny, but unsuccessful, Lister-Climax car built for Formula 2 racing in 1957

below Graham Hill in the Lola Type 90 which won the Indianapolis 500 Mile Race in 1966 under the name of the Red Ball Special

Lola   England

Eric Broadley's first special was an 1172-cc sports car with a Ford 10 engine. As the Lola it was put into limited production, primarily for racing, and expanded into a very successful Coventry-Climax-powered sports/racing car. In 1960 Broadley entered into the field of single-seaters with a front-engined Formula Junior car, but the following year he went the Cooper-route with a rear-engined car for the same Formula, using a Ford engine. In 1962 the

Bowmaker hire-purchase firm formed a racing team and financed Lola to build Formula 1 cars, using V8 Coventry-Climax engines. The chassis was a logical development of the Formula Junior cars, the engine being behind the driver, driving to an Italian-built gearbox and final drive. Suspension was independent all-round and the chassis was a tubular space-frame.

From these beginnings Broadley expanded the Lola firm to build cars for every possible single-seater Formula, keeping well clear of becoming involved with their own works team, but working in close co-operation with their customers. From space-frame cars Lola moved to aluminium monocoque chassis frames and their products ranged from Formule Vee to Indianapolis cars. They have been successful in almost every Formula for which they have built cars. There was a brief sortie into Formula 1 with Honda and later with Graham Hill's Embassy team, but generally speaking Formula 1 has been carefully avoided by Lola. The firm has generated its own market and is possibly the biggest racing-car manufacturer of all time, though always with proprietary engines and gearboxes, the chassis, suspension and bodywork being the Lola portion. Lola cars are serialized by a T-number, the first two figures denoting the design number and the third being the Mark number of that design. This has included all cars, from single-seaters to quasi-road-going racing coupés.

The Lola Type 370 built for the Embassy racing team for Formula 1 in 1974. From this car Graham Hill evolved his own Formula 1 car

Year: 1962
Model: Mark IV
Engine: Coventry-Climax
Number of cylinders: 8 in-vee
Bore and Stroke: 63 × 60 mm
Capacity: 1494 cc
Valves: Inclined overhead with two ohcs per bank
Induction: Down-draught carburettors
Wheelbase: 7 ft 6 in
Forward Speeds: 5
Front Suspension: Wishbones, radius arms and coil spring
Rear Suspension: Wishbones, radius rods and coil spring
Chassis Frame: Tubular space-frame
Maximum Speed: 160 mph

Year: 1966
Model: Type 90
Engine: Ford
Number of cylinders: 8 in-vee
Bore and stroke: 95·5 × 72·9 mm
Capacity: 4175 cc
Valves: Inclined overhead with two ohcs per bank
Induction: Fuel-injection

Wheelbase: 8 ft 6 in
Forward Speeds: 2—Hewland
Front Suspension: Rocker arm and wishbone with inboard coil spring
Rear Suspension: Transverse links, radius rods and coil springs
Chassis Frame: Aluminium monocoque
Maximum Speed: 195 mph

Lotus
England

The name Lotus first appeared shortly after the war when Colin Chapman built himself an Austin 7 trials car, and christened it Lotus, after the lotus blossom, which is said to induce drowsiness—for after many all-night sessions of work to get the car finished this was the state to which he and his friends had been reduced. From here Chapman went on to build Austin 7 racing/sports cars and with these he went from strength to strength, using more and more powerful engines, such as Ford and MG, until he arrived at the stage where he could use a Coventry-Climax engine. When the racing Formula 2 was laid down in 1957 Chapman was quick to join in with a single-seater Climax-powered Lotus which was very small and very light. Weight saving became one of his greatest studies, along with the desire to make every component do more than one job. Although successful these early Formula 2 Lotus cars were no match for their keen rival, the Cooper-Climax, and as Chapman progressed he fitted larger and larger Climax engines, until he was taking part in Formula 1 races. Even with 2·5-litre Climax engines the Lotus cars were

Alan Stacey driving a Lotus 16 in the 1959 British GP at Aintreee where he finished 8th

top left Trevor Taylor driving a Lotus 25 in the 1963 German GP seen at the Flugplatz
top right Graham Hill finishing 2nd in the 1968 German GP in a Lotus 49
far right The 1968 Lotus 56 turbine car for Indianapolis – driver Graham Hill

never quite the equal of Coopers using the same power unit—though they had superior road-holding, they lacked reliability.

Chapman kept to his front-engined design throughout 1957, 1958 and 1959, the last of the series being a beautiful example of streamlined shape. So small were these cars that the drivers had some difficulty in getting into the cockpit, and though they were still very light and held the road well, they were not in the forefront of GP racing. Finally Chapman joined the Cooper school of thought whereby the engine should be mounted behind the driver and not in front, and the 1960 Lotus cars were fine examples of a purely functional racing car, not pretty to look at but remarkably effective. They were very low, very light and had the driver sitting in front of the engine, with his feet between the front wheels. In 1960 these rear-engined Lotus cars appeared in Formula 1 and Formula 2 guise, with Coventry-Climax engines, and in Formula Junior form with Ford 105E engines. The Formula 1 cars won the GP of Monaco and the American GP, as well as many other important races, while the Lotus Juniors were almost unbeatable in their class. For 1961 a sleeker version of the rear-engined car was produced and many of the technical innovations of these cars were copied quite blatantly by other racing-car designers.

With the introduction of the Coventry-Climax V8 engine for Formula 1 racing, Chapman squeezed it into virtually the same chassis that had taken the 4-cylinder engine, and in 1962 produced a car that was to set a fashion that was copied by almost everyone. This was the Lotus 25 'monocoque' chassis, constructed from sheet aluminium, rivetted into a box form and doing away with all tubes. Until this point Chapman had led the design world with his pure tubular space-frames. The 'monocoque' structure which was light, strong and easy to fabricate, set a fashion in racing-car design that is still

with us today. This concept kept the name Lotus in the forefront of racing throughout the days of the 1½-litre Formula. In 1967 he created another landmark in racing-car design, with the Lotus 49. This was designed around the Ford-Cosworth DFV-V8 engine for the 3-litre Formula, and used the engine as part of the chassis. The cockpit comprised a sheet-aluminium 'monocoque' tube, with the front suspension mounted at one end and the engine at the other. The gearbox and rear suspension were attached to the back of the engine and it was the cylinder block that held the car together. This new Lotus was an immediate success, and the following year, when the Cosworth V8 became available to other designers, they naturally followed the concept started by Chapman.

The Lotus designers had also been building cars for the various smaller Formulae, based on production Ford engines, but as Formula 1 became more competitive and sophisticated, Lotus phased out the building of production racing cars and concentrated on Formula 1 cars for their own team. In 1970 the Lotus 49 was superseded by the Lotus 72, again innovative and having torsion-bar suspension in place of coil springs, and having all the disc brakes mounted inboard on the sprung mass of the car.

Interspersed in this activity was a busy programme of cars for the Indianapolis 500 Mile Race, sponsored by the Ford Motor Company and later by the STP concern. With the Lotus 38 Chapman revolutionized the track-racing scene in America, producing a relatively small and compact rear-engined car that eventually set the standards for all future Indy cars. This first Indy Lotus used a pushrod ohv Ford V8 engine giving 350 bhp and weighing 350 lb, a requirement that Chapman demanded of the Detroit engineers before he would even contemplate building the car. This was followed by the more powerful four ohc racing Ford V8 and after this term with Ford, Chapman moved into a new realm altogether with Andy Granatelli and his STP team. This was the gas turbine-powered racing car, already begun by Granatelli. The Lotus 56 was the outcome and by this time aerodynamics were playing a big part in these 190-mph cars, so the new Lotus was wedge-shaped to utilize the air flow to provide down-thrust. The STP Lotus projects were fraught with problems and troubles and did not achieve the success that was due to them. In 1971 Chapman turned some of the knowledge gained with the Pratt & Whitney gas turbine Indy car towards Formula 1, with the Lotus 56B which was a road-racing version, with 4-w-d. Shortly before this Lotus had been among the most successful with the adaptation of 4-w-d to GP racing, with the Lotus 63, using a mid-mounted Cosworth V8 engine. All these interesting projects were really offshoots from the main stream, which was the Lotus 49/72 concept which had become 'orthodox'.

Since the Lotus 72, subsequent Lotus designs have been developments of this, with the accent on detail innovations rather than any radically new concept, which can be seen to be due to the continued use of the successful Cosworth V8 engine. Using that compact and efficient power-pack it is difficult not to design a Formula 1 car that does not owe something to the Lotus 49 of 1967. The latest in the long line of Lotus racing cars is the Lotus 78, which brings some new thinking on aerodynamics to the racing-car scene.

Year: 1958
Model: Type 16—Formula 2
Engine: Coventry-Climax (front mounted)
Number of cylinders: 4
Bore and Stroke: 81·9 × 71·1 mm
Capacity: 1475 cc
Valves: Inclined overhead with two ohcs
Induction: Horizontal carburettors
Wheelbase: 7 ft 4 in
Forward Speeds: 5-Lotus
Front Suspension: Independent by lower wishbone, upper transverse link, anti-roll bar, coil spring
Rear Suspension: Independent by Chapman coil spring strut, radius arm and drive shaft
Chassis Frame: Tubular space-frame
Maximum Speed: 140 mph

Year: 1962
Model: Type 25—Formula 1
Engine: Coventry-Climax (rear mounted)
Number of cylinders: 8 in-vee
Bore and Stroke: 63 × 60 mm
Capacity: 1494 cc
Valves: Inclined overhead with two ohcs per bank
Induction: Down-draught carburettors
Wheelbase: 7 ft 7 in
Forward Speeds: 5
Front Suspension: Lower wishbone, upper rocker arm, inboard coil spring
Rear Suspension: Lower wishbone, upper transverse link, radius rods and coil spring
Chassis Frame: Aluminium monocoque
Maximum Speed: 160 mph

Year: 1965
Model: Type 38—Indianapolis
Engine: Ford—USA
Number of cylinders: 8 in-vee
Bore and Stroke: 95·5 × 72·9 mm
Capacity: 4175 cc
Valves: Four per cylinder, two ohcs per bank
Induction: Fuel-injection
Wheelbase: 8 ft 0 in
Forward Speeds: 2

Front Suspension: Lower wishbone, upper rocker arm, inboard coil spring; right-hand suspension longer than left
Rear Suspension: Lower wishbone, upper transverse link, radius rods, coil spring; right-hand suspension longer than left
Chassis Frame: Aluminium monocoque
Maximum Speed: 180 mph

Year: 1970
Model: Type 72—Formula 1
Engine: Cosworth DFV
Number of cylinders: 8 in-vee
Bore and Stroke: 85·6 × 64·8 mm
Capacity: 2993 cc
Valves: Four per cylinder, two ohcs per bank
Induction: Lucas fuel-injection
Wheelbase: 8 ft 4 in

Forward Speeds: 5 Hewland
Front Suspension: Wishbones and torsion bars
Rear Suspension: Wishbones, radius rods, torsion bars
Chassis Frame: Aluminium monocoque; engine a stressed member
Maximum Speed: 185 mph

Year: 1977
Model: Type 78—Formula 1
Engine: Cosworth DFV
Number of cylinders: 8 in-vee
Bore and Stroke: 85·6 × 64·8 mm
Capacity: 2993 cc
Valves: Four per cylinder, two ohcs per bank
Induction: Lucas fuel-injection
Wheelbase: 9 ft 0 in
Forward Speeds: 5 or 6 Hewland
Front Suspension: Lower wishbone upper rocker arm, inboard coil spring
Rear Suspension: Transverse links, radius rods, coil springs
Chassis Frame: Aluminium monocoque; engine a stressed member
Maximum Speed: 190 mph

The aerodynamic Lotus 78 driven by Mario Andretti in the 1977 Monaco GP

Maki

Japan

The Maki was very much a 'stranger from the East'; the small Japanese firm having built some not-too-successful Formula 3 cars, decided to enter European Formula 1 racing with a 'standard British Kit Car' design, using the Cosworth/Hewland mechanical package. It appeared for the 1974 season driven by Howden Ganley and suffered from being under-financed, with little expertise behind the design or operation. A structural failure caused its complete demise in practice for the German GP at the Nurburgring, and also inflicted severe injuries on the New Zealander. Happily, he recovered completely, which is more than can be said for the Maki car.

Howden Ganley practising for the British GP at Brands Hatch in 1974 with the Japanese Maki

Year: 1974
Model: F101
Engine: Cosworth DFV
Number of cylinders: 8 in-vee
Bore and Stroke: 85·6 × 64·8 mm
Capacity: 2993 cc
Valves: 4 per cylinder, two ohcs per bank
Induction: Lucas fuel-injection
Wheelbase: 8 ft 4 in

Forward Speeds: 5 Hewland
Front Suspension: Double wishbones and coil springs
Rear Suspension: Lower wishbone, transverse link, radius rods and coil springs
Chassis Frame: Aluminium monocoque; engine a stressed member
Maximum Speed: 170 mph

Maserati

Italy

The name Maserati is always associated with racing cars. Alfieri Maserati starting competitions in the early 1920s and by 1926 he had so transformed an 8-cylinder Diatto that it became the first Maserati racing car, a 1½-litre straight-8. The following year Alfieri and his brothers formed Fratelli Maserati, building racing cars and sports cars for customers and running factory cars themselves. They built supercharged 1½- and 2-litre racing cars, and in 1929 put two 2-litre 8-cylinder engines side-by-side in a chassis to produce their formidable pair of 16-cylinder *Formule Libre* racing cars that ran until 1934.

A programme of GP racing was carried out, with close co-operation between customers and the factory, and the 1930/2 supercharged 2½-litre 8-cylinder cars were very successful. When Alfieri died in 1932 his three brothers carried on the firm. After this they built narrow single-seater GP cars, which were one of the first European racing cars to have hydraulic brakes. For the 1934 Formula of 750 kg, the single-seater Maseratis of 1933 had to have artificial cockpit sides added to comply with the width rules. The new cars to this

An 8CM Maserati being driven into 3rd place in the 1935 French GP at Montlhéry by Geoffredo Zehender

8-cylinder pattern of 2·9 litres had wider chassis frames and 'stepped' body sides to comply with these regulations.

The factory followed the 8CM with a 3½-litre 6-cylinder version, known as the Tipo 34, and in 1935 they built a V8-cylinder car of over 4 litres, in a new chassis with torsion bar i.f.s. Like Bugatti and other small firms, Maserati could not match the German teams in GP racing and gradually turned their attention more and more to 'voiturette' racing, having already built 1100-cc 4-cylinder cars in 1934. In 1936 the 6CM appeared, with its torsion-bar i.f.s., supercharged twin-camshaft 6-cylinder engine and low build. They were made for sale to racing drivers, though often the works-supported cars, or experimental ones, were much faster than those sold to customers. In 1938/39 they built a 3-litre supercharged 8-cylinder car for GP racing, but though extremely fast this car was never reliable when trying to match Mercedes-Benz and Auto Union. One of these went to America in 1939 and driven by Wilbur Shaw won the Indianapolis 500 Mile Race. It repeated this performance in 1940. In that year Maserati produced a new 8-cylinder 3-litre, with 4 valves per cylinder, but Italy's involvement in the Second World War stopped the development of this car. In 'voiturette' racing they had changed in 1938 from the 6CM to the 4CL, this being a supercharged 4-cylinder engine with twin ohcs, of square bore/stroke ratio, measuring 78 × 78 mm. It had 4 valves per cylinder, and was known as the 16-valve Maserati. It was this engine that was 'doubled-up' in the last pre-war 8-cylinder.

In 1946 the 4CL Maserati was in the forefront of racing, and the brothers developed this car into the 4CLT models, with two-stage supercharging and

J.M. Fangio cornering in a Maserati 4CLT/48 during his successful European season in 1948

tubular chassis frames. At all times the i.f.s. had been by wishbones and torsion bars, with quarter-elliptic rear springs carrying a rigid axle. In 1947 Fratelli Maserati sold out to the Orsi family, and the firm moved from Bologna to Modena, Cav. Orsi and his son Omer keeping the name Maserati and the badge of the Trident of Bologna. The 4CLT was redesigned, with coil-spring front suspension and improved chassis frame and labelled the 4CLT/48; many were sold to customers and raced alongside the factory team. The new Maserati factory cars stayed in GP racing until 1950, by which time the 4CLT/48 was outclassed. They returned to racing in 1952 with unsupercharged 6-cylinder 2-litre cars for the Formula 2 and were soon back on form, being chief rivals to Ferrari. This car was developed through 1953 and much of the knowledge went into their new car for the 1954 Formula 1 racing—the 250F. This was one of their most successful models, with coil-spring i.f.s., tubular space-frame, de Dion rear axle with the gearbox integral with the final drive unit and mounted transversely, and 2½-litre unsupercharged engine. Continuing their policy of making production racing cars, the 250F was on sale and four came to England, for Moss, Salvadori, Bira and BRM. The 250F was notable for the fact that it won the first race for which it was entered, the 1954 Argentine GP, driven by Fangio.

Development of the 250F continued through 1954–7, the factory cars being the most successful in 1957, while private owners notched up many victories. A very powerful V12-cylinder engine of 2½ litres, was built to fit into a modified 250F frame, and began to show its paces in 1957, but a series of financial disasters forced the Maserati firm to withdraw from racing before it caused their complete downfall. They continued to build racing cars to special order, but no longer ran a works team, and 1958 saw the last of Maserati in GP racing. Among these special projects was a car for the Eldorado Ice Cream Company designed for the Monza banked-track racing. Stirling Moss drove it. This was a large and strong 250F, with a 4·2-litre V8 sports-car engine suitably modified, and a 2-speed gearbox. It was a big husky car and as fast as most of the Indianapolis cars of the time, producing over 400 bhp.

Maserati's interest in racing never really stopped, for although they turned to production GT cars, they were always producing experimental engines or cars and in 1966 they became involved with the Cooper Car Company, supplying them with 3-litre versions of the V12-cylinder engine of 1957 and running a development programme for them. In 1969 the Orsi family sold the firm to the French Citroën Company, for the purpose of making V6 Maserati engines for the SM-Citroën. In 1975 Citroën closed down the Modena plant, even though Maserati GT cars were still being built. However, the Maserati was not going to die as easily as that and Italian finances resurrected the production of GT cars, though racing Maseratis are not likely to be seen again.

Stirling Moss at Silverstone in his newly acquired Maserati 250F in 1954

Year: 1934
Model: 8CM
Engine: Maserati
Number of cylinders: 8 in-line
Bore and Stroke: 69 × 100 mm
Capacity: 2992 cc
Valves: Inclined overhead with two ohcs

Induction: Supercharged
Wheelbase: 8 ft 6¾ in (2570 mm)
Forward Speeds: 4
Front and Rear Suspension: Semi-elliptic leaf springs
Chassis-Frame: Channel-section
Maximum Speed: 145 mph

Year: 1936
Model: 6CM
Engine: Maserati
Number of cylinders: 6
Bore and Stroke: 65 × 75 mm
Capacity: 1493 cc
Valves: Inclined overhead with two ohcs
Induction: Supercharged

Wheelbase: 8 ft 1 in (2490 mm)
Forward Speeds: 4
Front Suspension: Independent by transverse arms and torsion bars
Rear Suspension: Semi-elliptic leaf springs
Chassis Frame: Channel-section
Maximum Speed: 135 mph

Year: 1948
Model: 4CLT/48
Engine: Maserati
Number of cylinders: 4
Bore and Stroke: 78 × 78 mm
Capacity: 1490 cc
Valves: Inclined overhead with two ohcs
Induction: Two-stage supercharging

Wheel base: 8 ft $1\frac{1}{2}$ in (2500 mm)
Forward Speeds: 4
Front Suspension: Independent by transverse rocker arm compressing coil spring and lower wishbone
Rear Suspension: Rigid axle, quarter-elliptic leaf springs
Chassis Frame: Tubular
Maximum Speed: 155 mph

Year: 1954/57
Model: 250F
Engine: Maserati
Number of cylinders: 6
Bore and Stroke: 84 × 75 mm
Capacity: 2493 cc
Valves: Inclined overhead with two ohcs
Induction: Three double-choke Weber carburettors

Wheelbase: 7 ft $5\frac{3}{4}$ in (2280 m)
Forward Speeds: 4 or 5
Front Suspension: Independent by double wishbones and coil springs
Rear Suspension: de Dion with transverse leaf spring
Chassis Frame: Tubular space-frame
Maximum Speed: 170 mph

Maserati-Milan   Italy

In 1949 the Maserati 4CLT/48 was reaching the end of its useful life as a front-rank GP contender, and when the Automobile Club of Milan offered substantial sums of money for any new cars appearing in the Italian GP, a Milan Scuderia run by the Ruggeri brothers decided to do something about it. With Mario Speluzzi they modified two 4CLT/48 Maseratis sufficiently to justify the name Maserati-Milan and claim the monies. Speluzzi had been doing development work on the Maserati engine for speedboat use, and this was employed to good effect in the new cars, his two-stage supercharger layout giving 44 lb/in^2 boost, while he also designed new brakes. Driven by

Farina and Taruffi, the cars were quite fast but unreliable, but development continued.

In 1950 the Scuderia Milan built an entirely new chassis of tubular construction, with wishbone and torsion bar i.f.s. and de Dion rear axle, on one car, and i.r.s. by trailing links on another. The engine was the Speluzzi-built Maserati 1½-litre, while gearbox and differential unit were Maserati. The Milan cars, as they were now called, raced during 1950 but without success, the project being more costly and complicated than the Scuderia Milan could really afford. They faded out in 1951, but were remembered for the sheer volume of sound that came from the exhaust pipe of that highly supercharged engine.

Juan Jover driving the Milan car in the 1950 Spanish GP at Barcelona, on the Pedrables circuit

Year: 1950
Model: F1
Engine: Maserati-Milan
Number of cylinders: 4
Bore and Stroke: 78 × 78 mm
Capacity: 1490 cc
Valves: Inclined overhead with two ohcs
Induction: Two-stage supercharging

Wheelbase: 8 ft 2¾ in
Forward Speeds: 4
Front Suspension: Independent by double wishbones and torsion bars
Rear Suspension: Independent by trailing arms and transverse leaf spring
Chassis Frame: Oval tubes
Maximum Speed: 160 mph

Maserati-Platé   Italy

When GP racing took to Formula 2 in 1952/3 Enrico Platé, owner of a small Scuderia running 4CLT/48 Maseratis, converted his cars to conform to the new rules of 2-litres unsupercharged. The 4-cylinder Maserati engines were

133

fitted with new cylinder blocks, of increased-bore and longer-stroke crankshafts. The superchargers were removed and two double-choke Weber carburettors fitted. The chassis was shortened and the radiator cowl modified, otherwise the bodywork was all Maserati.

Called Maserati-Platé, these two cars were regular competitors in Formula 2 racing during 1952, driven by Baron de Graffenried and Harry Schell. Though heavy by Formula 2 standards, they kept the Scuderia Platé in racing until Maserati produced some new cars. Long after being retired from racing the two cars were brought by 20th Century-Fox, at the instigation of de Graffenried and became the notorious 'Burano' GP cars in the film *Such Men Are Dangerous*. When the film was finished the cars were shipped to Hollywood to go into the film company's 'garage' of some 200 cars for use in film making.

Enrico Platé was killed in a pits accident during a race in the Argentine in 1954.

left Baron de Graffenried in one of the Maserati-Platé cars during the 1952 Swiss GP

right The bizarre March 711 run by the factory for the STP Racing Team in 1971

Year: 1952
Model: F2
Engine: Maserati
Number of cylinders: 4
Bore and Stroke: 84 × 90 mm
Capacity: 1995 cc
Valves: Inclined overhead with two ohcs
Induction: Two double-choke Weber carburettors

Wheelbase: 7 ft 6 in
Forward Speeds: 4
Front Suspension: Independent by transverse rocker arm compressing coil spring and lower wishbone
Rear Suspension: Rigid axle, quarter-elliptic leaf springs
Chassis Frame: Tubular
Maximum Speed: 135 mph

March
England

March Engineering came into being in a small way in 1969, building a Formula 3 car known as the March 693. This denoted the year of manufacture and the category for which the car was built, 1969 Formula 3, and most March cars have since followed this system. The firm started with a factory in Bicester for the express purpose of building racing cars for sale, relying on specialist engine firms for power units, and Hewland Engineering for gearboxes. The four men behind the project were Max Mosley (business), Alan Rees (team management), Graham Coaker (production) and Robin Herd (design), and the firm's name was derived from an amalgam of their initials, Mosley, Alan Rees, Coaker, Herd.

In 1970 they plunged into the world of Formula 1 with a simple and robustly designed car utilizing the Cosworth-Ford DFV engine. This was the March 701 and five of these were sold to customers, while the firm ran a pair of cars for STP. The first victory came from Jackie Stewart, driving a car for the Tyrrell Team. Other single-seaters were built for Formula 2 (702) and Formula 3 (703) and the supply of cars for the lesser Formulae has kept March Engineering in business ever since. They have continued to run a

Formula 1 factory team with sponsorship from outside. The 711 followed, which had a bizarre front aerofoil of elliptical shape; then followed the 721, an offshoot of which was the 721X which used an Alfa Romeo gearbox centrally placed between the engine and the rear axle but it was soon abandoned as a blind-alley of design. The 1972 cars started off badly and at mid-season a new car was hastily concocted using a 722 chassis, into which a Cosworth DFV was shoe-horned. The result was a small compact car that worked surprisingly well and in view of the speed of its design and construction it was called the 721G, the G being for the *Guinness Book of Records*, for March felt no Formula 1 car had ever been conceived so quickly!

This concoction was continued into the 731, the 741 and 751, the 1976 cars being revamped 1975 models. For 1977 the previous year's cars were modified and called 761B and experiments were carried out with a remarkable 6-wheeled car with two driving axles at the rear. All the Formula 1 cars have been powered by Cosworth DFV engines, apart from an abortive 711 that used an Alfa-Romeo V8 engine. Formula 2 March cars, powered by BMW engines have been particularly successful, winning the F2 European Championship, and in Formula 3 and other small-engined Formulae the March has been very successful and has proved an extremely saleable commodity.

The factory now concentrates on running its own Formula 1 team for outside sponsors, only selling Formula 1 cars after they have served their purpose as works cars, but the marketing of all other forms of single-seater continues unabated.

The successful works Formula 2 March-BMW 4-cylinder of 1973

Year: 1970
Model: 701
Engine: Cosworth DFV
Number of cylinders: 8 in-vee
Bore and Stroke: 85·6 × 64·8 mm
Capacity: 2993 cc
Valves: 4 per cylinder, two ohcs per bank
Induction: Lucas fuel-injection
Wheelbase: 7 ft 9 in

Forward Speeds: 5 Hewland
Front Suspension: Independent by double wishbones and coil springs
Rear Suspension: Independent by transverse link and wishbone, radius rods and coil springs
Chassis Frame: Aluminium monocoque; engine a stressed member
Maximum Speed: 170 mph

Year: 1976
Model: 761
Engine: Cosworth DFV
Number of cylinders: 8 in-vee
Bore and Stroke: 85·6 × 64·8 mm
Capacity: 2993 cc
Valves: 4 per cylinder, two ohcs per bank
Induction: Lucas fuel-injection
Wheelbase: 8 ft 4 in

Forward Speeds: 5 Hewland
Front Suspension: Double wishbones and coil springs
Rear Suspension: Transverse link, wishbone, radius rods, coil springs
Chassis Frame: Aluminium monocoque; engine a stressed member
Maximum Speed: 180 mph

Martini   France

Italian-born Renato (Tico) Martini grew up in Jersey and began work in a garage from where he built himself a special to join in the local motor racing. He came to prominence in 1962 at the Bouley Bay hillclimb with a Kart powered by a 650 cc Triumph motorcycle engine. The following year he moved to the Magny-Cours circuit in France to take charge of the workshops of the Winfield Racing School and took part in French club racing with Lotus, Cooper and Brabham cars, learning a lot about racing-car design while maintaining them himself. By mid-1967 he had decided that his future lay in building cars rather than racing them and he retired from active competition to build his first proper racing car, the MW 1 for Formula Ford. This serial prefix was Martini-Winfield for he was still closely associated with the school, though he formed a separate firm called Inter Auto, and his first job was to supply cars for the training school. These were simple and straightforward space-frame cars embodying much of what Martini had learnt from studying British car constructors' work. He also built a Formula 3 car for a tentative probe into that category and continued with it in 1969, though much of his time was taken up building cars for the new French Formule Renault—tiny single-seaters powered by Renault engines, for national racing.

Building school cars, Formula Renault cars and Formula 3 cars kept him busy for the next few years, and his Formula 3 cars became very successful in national racing, winning the French Championship in 1972 to begin a string of such successes. At this time he changed the serial numbers to MK for Martini-Knight (not an abbreviation of Mark), the second part being the name of the family who ran the Winfield School and had been so helpful, though the cars themselves were called Martini. With the various French national formulae keeping his small works busy and solvent Tico was able to expand into Formula 2 and in 1975 appeared the first 'monocoque' Martini, all previous cars having had tubular space-frames. This was the MK16 and with it Jacques Laffite won the European Formula 2 championship, using BMW power. In 1976 the MK19 was powered by a V6 Renault engine and one of these cars was runner-up in the Formula 2 European Championship. By this time Martini had built more than 200 cars and had established himself as a competent car constructor, entirely self-taught. His small works at Magny-Cours circuit was now unable to cope with the work coming in and a move was made to a new factory not far from the circuit, where Inter Auto continues to supply cars to the French sporting world for single-seater categories.

A Formula 1 project was underway in 1978 and the story of Tico Martini is as sound an approach to racing-car manufacture and participation as one could wish for. His steady and stolid progression is in sharp contrast to some people who have tried to start at the top and failed miserably.

Year: 1976
Model: MK19 Formula 2
Engine: Renault
Number of cylinders: 6 in vee
Bore and Stroke: 86 × 57·3 mm
Capacity: 1997 cc
Valves: 4 valves per cylinder. 4 ohcs
Induction: Fuel-injection
Wheelbase: 7 ft 11 in
Forward Speeds: 5 Hewland FG200
Front Suspension: Independent.
Double wishbones and coil springs
Rear Suspension: Independent.
Single transverse top link, twin
lower links, double radius rods and
coil springs
Chassis Frame: Monocoque
Maximum Speed: 160 mph

The MK19 Martini for Formula 2 in
1976 powered by a Renault V6
engine and driven to 3rd place in the
European Championship by Patrick
Tambay

Matra

France

The French aerospace firm of Engins Matra (Mecanique-Aviation-Traction)
looked for a diversion from the aircraft world and gave serious thought to
producing a high-performance luxury car, though it never materialized. They
decided the way into the automotive world was through racing and bought
up the small firm of Rene Bonnet, which got them into Formula 3. They
brought new standards of construction into racing cars—their monocoque
chassis frames were exceptionally good—and in 1966 they formed a liaison
with Ken Tyrrell to run Matra-Fords in Formula 3 and followed this with
Cosworth-engined cars in Formula 2. In 1967 the French Government and
the state-owned ELF petrol company gave Matra an enormous grant to

The 1970 Matra MS120 underoing initial testing at the Montlhéry track before
the start of the season

tackle Formula 1 which they did with a V12 engine, designed with a view to its ultimate use in a production road car, though this never materialized.

The works Matra V12 Formula 1 project never quite made the top class and many of its better efforts were overshadowed by the concurrent Matra-Cosworth V8 project run by Ken Tyrrell alongside the main factory team.

The Matra V12 engine was developed into a long-distance sports-car racing engine, and duly won the Le Mans 24-hour race, while in recent years it has been used in the Ligier car, the Matra firm withdrawing their racing team in 1973

Year: 1970
Model: MS 120—Formula 1
Engine: Matra
Number of cylinders: 12 in-vee
Bore and Stroke: 79·7 × 50 mm
Capacity: 3000 cc
Valves: 4 per cylinder, two ohcs per bank
Induction: Lucas fuel-injection

Wheelbase: 7 ft 11¾ in
Forward Speeds: 5 Hewland
Front Suspension: Double wishbones and coil springs
Rear Suspension: Transverse links, radius rods and coil springs
Chassis Frame: Aluminium monocoque
Maximum Speed: 175 mph

Matra-Cosworth Anglo–French

In 1968 when the Cosworth DFV Formula 1 engine became available to everyone, Ken Tyrrell persuaded the French aerospace firm Matra to build a Matra-Cosworth alongside their own V12-engined Formula 1 car. Jackie Stewart was extremely successful with the MS80 Cosworth-powered car, winning the World Championship in 1969 and gaining the Manufacturers' title for Matra. Although satisfying for the French firm, they would have preferred that he had been using their own V12 engine, but neither Stewart nor Tyrrell were convinced of its potential.

During 1969 Matra built Tyrrell a 4-wheel-drive car for experimental

Jackie Stewart driving the Matra Cosworth MS80 at Silverstone during the 1969 British GP which he won

purposes, called the MS84, and it had a tubular space-frame in contrast to all previous Matras which had had monocoque chassis frames. Like every 4-wheel-drive project at that time it never got the development it deserved and was abandoned. Tyrrell severed his connections with Matra in 1970, leaving them to go their own way with their V12 engines, and started his own racing-car building firm, using much of the knowledge he had gained from the French engineers.

Year: 1969
Model: MS80—Formula 1
Engine: Cosworth DFV
Number of cylinders: 8 in-vee
Bore and Stroke: 85·6 × 64·8 mm
Capacity: 2993 cc
Valves: 4 per cylinder, two ohcs per bank
Induction: Lucas fuel-injection
Wheelbase: 7 ft 10½ in

Forward Speeds: 5 Hewland
Front Suspension: Double wishbones and coil springs
Rear Suspension: Upper wishbone, lower links, radius rods and coil springs
Chassis Frame: Aluminium monocoque; engine a stressed member
Maximum Speed: 180 mph

Maybach Special   Australia

Europe is not the only continent where 'one-off' special racing cars are built. In Australia there was a real necessity for building one's own car as the importation of European cars was difficult. One of the most successful of the Australian specials in the post-war years was the Maybach Special built by Charlie Dean and his associates who worked for the Repco Engineering firm. This car was evolved over many years, using a 6-cylinder ex-German Army Maybach engine as the basis. The rugged ohc unit with inclined valves was heavy, but responsive to tuning.

The car was called the Maybach Special and was first built as a 2-seater sports car, using a home-made tubular ladder-frame. Studebaker independent front suspension, a Fiat 525 gearbox and a Lancia Lambda rear axle mounted on half-elliptic springs. It first appeared in 1946 in 3·8-litre form and was very active until the late '50s, during which time it changed owners three times and underwent so much development that there were actually four versions of the Maybach. In 1949 a 4·2-litre Maybach engine was installed and it was supercharged with a GMC-Roots blower, but in 1950 it ran un-blown with three marine Amal carburettors. Dean then sold it to Stan Jones (father of today's Formula 1 driver Alan Jones), but continued to look after the car and the development work with the backing of the Repco firm. In 1954 it was comprehensively rebuilt as a single-seater and after Jones crashed it badly it was redesigned completely with the engine mounted at an angle and the transmission offset to the right of the driver. The stroke of the engine was reduced from 110 mm to 100 mm to give 3·8-litres and Dean and Phil Irving designed a fuel-injection system for it. The semi-elliptic rear springs had already given way to quarter-elliptics with torque arms and the internals of the Fiat gearbox had been redesigned completely by the Repco engineers, as had most of the parts of the engine.

Jones raced it until it could no longer match the latest Maserati 250F cars that were finding their way to Australia, and the car then languished for two years. Ern Seelinger acquired it and gave it a new lease of life by installing a Chevrolet V8 engine of 4·6 litres and improving the front suspension and at the same time lengthening the chassis and fitting a de Dion rear suspension with a transverse leaf spring. In this Mark IV form it ran its last race in 1959. It is now being rebuilt to Mark III form with a Maybach engine once more.

When European cars and drivers first went to Australia after the war the Maybach was one of the few local specials to put up any sort of opposition to the latest cars from Surbiton or Modena.

The Maybach Special built by Charlie Dean and raced by Stan Jones in 1953/54 when it won the 1954 New Zealand GP. This is the Mark I in its third guise

Year: 1946–58
Model: Mark III
Engine: Maybach
Number of cylinders: 6 in-line
Bore and Stroke: 90 × 100 mm
Capacity: 3800 cc
Valves: Inclined overhead with single ohc
Induction: Carburettors
Wheelbase: 7 ft 11 in
Forward Speeds: 4
Front Suspension: Independent by wishbones and transverse leaf spring
Rear Suspension: Rigid axle on quarter-elliptic leaf springs
Chassis Frame: 4-in diameter tubular side-members
Maximum Speed: 145 mph

McLaren   New Zealand

Bruce McLaren learned the motor racing trade with the Cooper works team as number two to Jack Brabham and in 1966 he set out on his own, building his own Formula 1 car. Engines were a problem to start with and after abortive attempts with modified American Ford V8 Indianapolis engines, BRM V12 and Serenissima V8, the gate to progress was opened with the arrival of the Cosworth-Ford DFV. McLaren was soon into the business with the M7A, following the concepts set by the Lotus 49 and with designers Robin Herd and Gordon Coppuck, McLaren Racing improved rapidly, with McLaren himself directing design thoughts. As well as Formula 1 the firm competed in sports-car Can–Am racing and dabbled in Formula 2, but Bruce always felt that Formula 1 was the real pinnacle of motor racing, even though his cars were successful in American racing. The firm was a two-part affair, the English base at Colnbrook looking after European and worldwide racing, and a separate American branch concentrating on SCCA and USAC racing. When Robin Herd left to join the Cosworth firm, Coppuck took over as chief designer. Bruce McLaren was killed while testing a Can–Am car at Goodwood in 1970, but his wife and co-directors kept the firm going, though one basic need was lost. This was to give Bruce the satisfaction of seeing cars with his name on them, his ultimate dream having been to produce a road-going production GT car bearing the name McLaren.

Bruce McLaren driving an M7A car of his own construction and winning its first race at Brands Hatch in 1968

After his death the firm continued in racing, and concentrated on running a factory team as a profit-making business rather than a research and development department for other activities. From the first McLaren M1A a long list of cars has appeared, some very successful, some not so, and others downright failures, but in the overall scene the standing of McLaren cars is very high, especially in Formula 1 racing. None of the cars has been a particularly outstanding design, being functional and honest rather than 'clever' and the team led by Teddy Mayer won the Formula 1 World Championship in 1974 and 1976 with the McLaren M23. Like many teams they had a half-hearted try at 4-w-d in 1969 but soon abandoned it, though their efforts with turbo-charged Offenhauser engines for USAC racing has been very successful, McLaren cars winning the Indianapolis 500 in 1972, '74 and '76.

Year: 1970
Model: M14A Formula 1
Engine: Cosworth DFV
Number of cylinders: 8 in-vee
Bore and Stroke: 85·6 × 64·8 mm
Capacity: 2993 cc
Valves: Four per cylinder, two ohcs per bank
Induction: Lucas fuel-injection
Wheelbase: 7 ft 11 in
Forward Speeds: 5 Hewland DG300

Front Suspension: Independent by rocker-arm wishbones and inboard coil springs
Rear Suspension: Independent by transverse links, radius rods and coil springs
Chassis Frame: Aluminium monocoque; engine a stressed member
Maximum Speed: 175 mph

above An Indianapolis McLaren M16 of 1971 with turbo-charged Offenhauser engine driven by Mark Donohue

below The 1977 McLaren M26 Formula 1 car driven by James Hunt

Year: 1976
Model: M16E USAC
Engine: Offenhauser
Number of cylinders: 4
Bore and Stroke: 111·1 × 67·3 mm
Capacity: 2611 cc
Valves: Four per cylinder with twin ohcs
Induction: Turbo-charged
Wheelbase: 8 ft 10 in
Forward Speeds: 4 Hewland LG500
Front Suspensions: Independent by rocker arm wishbones and inboard coil springs
Rear Suspension: Independent by transverse link and wishbone, radius rods and coil springs
Chassis Frame: Aluminium monocoque
Maximum Speed: 195 mph

McNamara   America/Germany

American serviceman Francis McNamara started competitive driving while with the US Forces in Germany and, caught by the racing-car bug, he left the army and set up a small factory at Lenggries, in Southern Germany, a part of the country he knew well and liked. This was in the late '60s and Formula Vee was flourishing in Germany so McNamara was soon building FV cars for sale and running a successful works entry in national racing. His firm also did general tuning work, race preparation and was involved with official Ford saloon-car racing on the preparation and development side.

From Formula Vee the McNamara firm moved into Formula 3, with continued success, the design work started by Dan Hawkes was continued by the Austrian Josef Karasek, who had spent some time in the Lola design office working for Eric Broadley.

In 1970 the Granatelli family visited Lenggries on behalf of their STP Corporation and commissioned McNamara Racing KG to build some cars for Mario Andretti to race in the Indianapolis 500 and other USAC events. This was initiated by Bill Dunne, the European STP competitions manager, who had seen the F3 McNamara cars at the Nurburgring and elsewhere and was prepared to give them a go in preference to an established 'big name' constructor, an avenue already well explored by STP. Karasek was delighted with the opportunity, having had experience with the Indianapolis Lola projects, and the prototype car was ready for testing in April, while a brand-new car was prepared for the 500 Mile Race in May, where it finished 6th. They built new cars for the 1971 season, still using turbo-charged Ford V8 engines, and though the 1971 design won the SAE award for the outstanding engineering contribution in the field of racing car design for the Indianapolis 500 Mile Race, it did not achieve success in the event, and the whole Indy project foundered in a sea of litigation between McNamara and the Granatellis.

Returning to their Southern German base, McNamara and Karasek continued their business until McNamara's wife died suddenly and this upset him so much that he folded up his factory and returned to America. Karasek remained in Germany and continued to design competition cars on his own.

Year: 1969 Formula 3
Model: Sebring Mk 3
Engine: Ford-Holbay
Number of cylinders: 4
Bore and Stroke: 80·1 × 48·4 mm
Capacity: 997 cc
Valves: Pushrod overhead
Induction: Carburettor
Wheelbase: 7 ft 8 in

Forward Speeds: 4 Hewland
Front Suspension: Independent by wishbones and coil springs
Rear Suspension: Independent by transverse links, radius arms and coil springs
Chassis Frame: Tubular space-frame
Maximum Speed: 135 mph

Mario Andretti testing the 1970 STP-McNamara Indy car prior to the 500 Mile Race

Year: 1970 USAC
Model: T-500
Engine: Ford
Number of cylinders: 8 in-vee
Bore and Stroke: 95·5 × 45·7 mm
Capacity: 2619 cc
Valves: Overhead with two ohcs per bank
Induction: Fuel injection with turbo-charger

Wheelbase: 8 ft 0 in
Forward Speeds: 4 Hewland LG500
Front Suspension: Independent by double wishbones and coil springs
Rear Suspension: Independent by double wishbones and coil springs
Chassis Frame: Aluminium monocoque with tubular engine cradle
Maximum Speed: 190 mph

Mercédès-Benz   Germany

The history of Mercédès-Benz cars in racing can be traced back to the beginning of the motor vehicle, for Gottlieb Daimler was among the first to build a motor vehicle, and a Daimler engine powered the Panhard that won the first motor race in 1895. A contemporary of Daimler, Carl Benz, also built cars from the very beginning, and these two German firms progressed in parallel, though Daimler was undoubtedly the more successful of the two. Until the end of the 19th century, motor vehicles had but one form, and racing cars were merely superior production cars, but it was Daimler who was the first to build one of his Cannstatt-Daimler cars especially for competition purposes. In 1901 the Daimler cars were changed in name to Mercédès, for trade purposes, and they built up a name in racing in the Gordon Bennett series, with more and more specialized cars, the gap between the racing car and the production car was widening rapidly.

The firm made numerous onslaughts in GP racing during the Edwardian period, notably with their 1908 GP car and even more successful 1914 GP

Mercédès. The 1908 car was a 12·8-litre 4-cylinder side-valve with high-tension magneto ignition in use for the first time. The 1914 car was much more advanced, and was one of the milestones in motor-racing history. It was of 4½ litres, with 4-cylinders and an ohc operating inclined valves through rockers, the design being closely tied up with Daimler aero engines. It was the 1914 team of GP Mercédès which first approached motor racing as a technical exercise rather than a sport. This racing programme of research and development continued in 1921 and through the early GP years of the 1920s, the cars using 2-litre and 1½-litre engines as the Formulae demanded. In 1926 the Daimler Company amalgamated with the Benz Company, to form Daimler-Benz Aktiengesellschaft, and the cars were called Mercédès-Benz. The racing department followed the trends of Daimler rather than Benz, which was unfortunate as Benz had been developing a mid-engined racing car that was over thirty years ahead of its time.

In the lean years of the late '20s they raced with stripped sports cars, and Daimler-Benz AG were limited in their activities. In 1934, when GP racing took on a new lease of life, Daimler-Benz threw their full weight into racing. From 1934 to 1939, apart from 1936, they led the field in GP racing and development, so much so that most of their rivals fell by the wayside and withdrew. The 1937 W125 Mercédès-Benz was the pinnacle of brute-force racing, the 5·66-litre straight-8-cylinder engine giving nearly 600 bhp. In 1939 they used two-stage supercharging on their 3-litre cars, and engine and chassis efficiency improved rapidly, while 1939 saw the W165 model run in one race, in which they finished 1st and 2nd, this being the V8-cylinder 1½-litre 'voiturette' that surprised the Italians.

In 1954 Mercédès-Benz cars returned to GP racing, after getting the racing department into action with the 300SL sports car in 1952, and the 2½-litre W196 car was outstanding from a mechanical point of view. It had fuel-injection and desmodromic valve gear on its straight-8-cylinder engine, fully independent suspension to all four wheels by torsion bars, a 5-speed all-syncromesh gearbox and a fully enveloping streamlined body. These cars were 1st and 2nd in their first race, the French GP of 1954, and in 1955

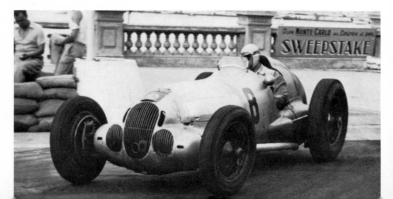

the pace of mechanical development set by Daimler-Benz left everyone behind, rather as it had done in 1938/39. Before everyone was forced to give up GP racing in despair, Daimler-Benz withdrew and turned the competition department back to production experimental work. Mercédès-Benz won the Manufacturers' Award in 1954 and 1955, as well as providing the car for Fangio, the champion driver of those two years.

A visit to the Daimler-Benz museum at the Stuttgart factory will convince anyone that the firm are essentially engine builders, carrying on the traditions of Gottlieb Daimler, and it is interesting that since 1955 there have been persistent rumours that Daimler-Benz would return to GP racing, but nothing has ever materialized.

Year: 1937
Model: W125
Engine: Daimler-Benz M125
Number of cylinders: 8 in-line
Bore and Stroke: 94 × 102 mm
Capacity: 5660 cc
Valves: Inclined overhead with two ohcs
Induction: Supercharged

Wheelbase: 9 ft 2 in
Forward Speeds: 4
Front Suspension: Independent by wishbones and coil springs
Rear Suspension: de Dion with torsion bars
Chassis Frame: Oval-section tubes
Maximum Speed: 195 mph

Year: 1954
Model: W196
Engine: Daimler-Benz M196
Number of cylinders: 8 in-line
Bore and Stroke: 76 × 68·8 mm
Capacity: 2496 cc
Valves: Inclined overhead, 'desmodromic' with two ohcs
Induction: Bosch fuel-injection
Wheelbase: 7 ft 8½ in

Forward Speeds: 5
Front Suspension: Independent by wishbones and torsion bars
Rear Suspension: Independent by low-pivot swing axles and torsion bars
Chassis Frame: Tubular space-frame
Maximum Speed: 175 mph

left Rudolf Caracciola rounding the Gasworks Hairpin in a Mercédès-Benz W125 during the 1937 Monaco GP

right J.M. Fangio in a Mercédès-Benz W196 during the 1954 German GP at the Nurburgring

MG   England

Although the MG Car Company of Abingdon made competition cars from
the introduction of their first Midget, in 1928, it was not until they were about
to give up competition that they marketed a single-seater racing car. This
was the unorthodox R-type of 1935 that was introduced just before Managing
Director Cecil Kimber announced that the MG firm would no longer support
racing. They had always marketed 2-seater sports/racing cars that could be
converted into pure racing cars, and sold some chassis to specialist firms
who built single-seater bodies on them. The R-type was sold as a ready-to-
race single-seater car, and had an unusual Y-shaped chassis frame made from
welded sheet steel, a highly supercharged 750-cc 4-cylinder engine, preselector gearbox, all-round independent suspension by wishbones and torsion
bars, and a very slim body. A number of these R-types were sold and they
raced quite successfully once the drivers had become used to the violent roll
experienced on sharp corners. Three of these cars were modified by McEvoy-
Pomeroy Ltd. to having twin ohc cylinder heads, which gave more power
than the single-cam MG head, but lost in more weight and less reliability.

Apart from the R-type there were MG Specials of pure racing nature built
around the 4-cylinder Midget and 6-cylinder Magnette chassis. The 750-cc
J4 and Q-type Midgets were most suitable for conversion into single-seaters,
as was the supercharged K3 model Magnette. The 1100-cc 6-cylinder K3
models were very successful as road-racing specials, track specials and hill-
climb cars, the names of H.C. Hamilton, R.T. Horton and E.R. Hall springing
to mind as specialists in these fields. Fast single-seater Q-types were built
for Brooklands racing, and one of the fastest was that built for George
Harvey-Noble by R.R. Jackson, a great MG specialist, this car lapping
Brooklands at 122·4 mph. Practically every British driver of note in the
mid-'30s drove an MG at some time or another.

With no track racing for the specialized MGs after the war, many of them
were converted back to sports cars. In their hey-day the racing Magnettes
in single-seater form were numerous, and Capt. G.E.T. Eyston used his for
record breaking as well as road racing and track racing. The MG firm always
took an interest in record breaking, and the Magic Midget was the first
750-cc car to achieve 120 mph. Eyston's Magic Magnette and 'Goldie'
Gardner's record-breaking cars made history in the '30s. After the war the
MG Car Company continued to support Gardner and his record-breaking
MGs using post-war pushrod engines, and they also built a very fine Bonne-
vile record-breaking 'teardrop' with a supercharged 1½-litre 'twin-cam' MG
engine that took records at over 250 mph.

In their own sphere, namely the 750-cc, 1100-cc and 1500-cc categories,
the MG Car Company has done more for British prestige in racing and
record breaking than almost anyone.

Year: 1933
Model: K3 Magnette
Engine: M.G.
Number of cylinders: 6
Bore and Stroke: 57 × 71 mm
Capacity: 1087 cc
Valves: Overhead with single ohc
Induction: Supercharged
Wheelbase: 7 ft $10\frac{3}{16}$ in
Forward Speeds: 4 ENV
preselector
Front and Rear Suspension: Semi-
elliptic leaf springs
Chassis Frame: Channel-section
Maximum Speed: 125 mph

Richard Seaman in his K3 MG
Magnette during the Coppa Acerbo
'voiturette' race at Pescara in 1934

The all-independently sprung, back-bone chassis, R-type MG Midget
of 1935.

Year: 1935
Model: R-type Midget
Engine: M.G.
Number of cylinders: 4
Bore and Stroke: 57 × 73 mm
Capacity: 746 cc
Valves: Overhead with single ohc
Induction: Supercharged
Wheelbase: 7 ft 6 in

Forward Speeds: 4 ENV preselector
Front and Rear Suspension:
Independent by double wishbones
and torsion bars
Chassis Frame: Y-shaped box-
section
Maximum Speed: 120 mph

Multi-Union Anglo–Italian

In 1936 C.S. Staniland, the Fairey Aviation test pilot, was racing a Tipo B Alfa Romeo 2·9-litre and the following year the car underwent a complete rebuild. A special 4-speed gearbox replaced the 3-speed Alfa Romeo, Lockheed hydraulic brakes were made, more power obtained from the engine and a new body was built on the style of the GP Mercedes-Benz, the car being named Multi-Union. The whole cost was borne by Jack Emmott and W.C. Deveraux of High Duty Alloys.

Staniland drove the car in 1938 and won the Phoenix Park Race at 97·54 mph and a Brooklands Outer Circuit handicap race at 127·77 mph, followed by another similar race at 133·26 mph, during which he lapped at 141 mph. The car was remarkably adaptable to all types of racing, from the fast-banked track, reaching 160 mph down the Railway Straight, to road circuits such as the Campbell Circuit and Donington Park. At the end of the season Staniland took Class D International records for 5 kilometres and 5 miles, 10 kilometres and 10 miles, at 139·5, 139·9, 139·6 and 138·9 mph, respectively, all made on the Brooklands Outer Circuit. He also took the Class D Brooklands lap record at 141·45 mph.

For the 1939 season the car underwent another and more major rebuild, emerging for the last Brooklands meeting ever to be held, and in its new form it was known as Multi-Union II. Little remained of the original Alfa Romeo, apart from the engine, the chassis sidemembers and rear axle. It now had larger superchargers, different carburettors, and was producing much more power than before; the divided propshaft rear axle was retained, as was the fuel tank. The Alfa Romeo front axle was removed and Tecnauto i.f.s. fitted, trailing links operating coil springs in torsion. The rear axle was mounted on coil springs instead of leaf springs, and located by a Panhard rod, and larger hydraulic brakes were fitted. Hydraulic shock-absorbers were used which were controlled from the cockpit and a hydraulic throttle control was used. All this use of hydraulics was instigated by Lockheeds. It had a new and sleeker bodywork, still on Mercedes-Benz lines.

Staniland started with a race on the Campbell circuit and then ran in a Mountain Circuit race, but the engine started to give trouble so an official attempt on the Outer Circuit lap record had to be abandoned. It ran in one outer circuit race, firing on seven cylinders, and lapped at over 140 mph, finishing 4th. Had it attempted the lap record at the beginning of the meeting it would undoubtedly have beaten Cobb's 143·44 mph. That a road-racing car was so fast on the bumpy banked track confounded the track *habitués*, who had maintained that a heavy car with an engine of 8 litres or more was necessary for 142-mph laps. The Multi-Union had been achieving it on 2·9 litres.

After the war G.F. Yates bought the car and made a brief appearance with it and then abandoned the idea of racing it; after lying dormant for many years it changed hands and re-appeared in VSCC racing, but the cylinder blocks were showing signs of old age and it never ran properly. It has now been rebuilt once more with specially made cast-iron cylinder blocks to replace the original alloy ones. This was one of the more successful and scientific 'specials', as it was a better Tipo B Alfa Romeo than Alfa Romeo had made originally.

The Multi-Union in its original form, driven by Chris Staniland at Brooklands on the Campbell road circuit in 1938

Year: 1939
Model: Multi-Union II
Engine: Alfa Romeo
Number of cylinders: 8 in-line
Bore and Stroke: 68·5 × 100 mm
Capacity: 2947 cc
Valves: Inclined overhead with two ohcs
Induction: Two superchargers

Wheelbase: 8 ft 10½ in
Forward Speeds: 4
Front Suspension: Independent by Tecnauto trailing arm and coil spring
Rear Suspension: Rigid axle on coil springs
Chassis Frame: Channel-section
Maximum Speed: 160 mph

Napier-Railton England

Built in 1933 by Thomson & Taylor Ltd. of Brooklands Track, to the special order of John Cobb, this vast car was designed specifically for track racing and record breaking, and at both it was highly successful. Reid Railton did the chassis design, using an underslung channel-section frame, with half-elliptic front springs, but double cantilever springs on each side at the rear. The engine was a 3-bank 12-cylinder Napier Lion aero engine, suitably modified for ground work. The huge engine had a bore and stroke of 139·7 × 130·2 mm, a capacity of 23,970 cc and developed 500 bhp at a leisurely 2200 rpm, the maximum speed of the car being about 170 mph on an axle ratio of 1·66 to 1.

It took numerous records at Montlhéry and Bonneville, including the 1 hour at 152·7 mph, and it broke the Brooklands lap record on many occasions, holding it ultimately at 143·44 mph. It was declared Brooklands Champion for 1934 and in 1937 earned the Brooklands Track Drivers' Star for John Cobb. For long-distance records it was fitted with three headlamps on a bar above the front cross-member and had a dynamo driven by a belt from the clutch shaft.

With such a huge reserve of power for the job in hand the Napier-Railton was one of the most reliable racing cars, and in 1935 it won the BRDC 500 Mile Race at 121·28 mph and in 1937 the same club's 500 Kilometer Race at 127·05 mph as well as winning shorter Brooklands handicap races, some at speeds well over 130 mph. Cobb eventually withdrew the car from Brooklands racing after 1937 as he was concentrating on the World's Land Speed Record with another car.

The car was carefully stored during the war and when Brooklands racing did not resume, the Napier-Railton was used for a film, featuring in *Pandora and Flying Dutchman*, somewhat modified as regards the bodywork. After that it was bought by GQ Parachutes Ltd. for use in practical testing of arrester-parachutes for bomber aircraft. The Napier-Railton was ideal for this job, with its great weight and power, and was used continually for 130-mph test runs. During this time it was fitted with disc brakes on the rear, as the drum brakes were somewhat primitive.

When GQ Parachutes had finished with the car it was sold to a member of the VSCC who ran it in some events, but it was not altogether suitable for circuit racing. It is still in the hands of a Vintage Club member and has been rebuilt to 'as new' condition.

John Cobb poses in the Napier-Railton outside the aeroplane sheds at Brooklands Track in 1933

Year: 1933
Model: Napier-Railton
Engine: Napier Lion
Number of cylinders: 12 in three banks of 4
Bore and Stroke: 139·7 × 130·2 mm
Capacity: 23,970 cc
Valves: Overhead with ohc on each bank
Induction: Carburettors

Wheelbase: 10 ft 10 in
Forward Speeds: 3
Front Suspension: Semi-elliptic leaf springs
Rear Suspension: Double cantilever leaf springs
Chassis Frame: Under-slung channel-section
Maximum Speed: 170 mph

Novi-Ferguson

Anglo–American

The last Indianapolis attempt using the powerful Novi V8 engine, was by the STP racing team in conjunction with Ferguson Research, the operation aimed at putting the vast power output through four tyres. Ferguson Research designed and built a complete chassis with all-round independent suspension and drive to all four wheels by the patented Ferguson system. It was one of the largest front-engined Indianapolis cars ever built and though fast, was more complicated and complex than the project justified. Two cars were built but neither was successful.

Year: 1964
Model: Indianapolis FF
Engine: Novi
Number of cylinders: 8 in-vee
Bore and Stroke: 80·2 × 66·7 mm
Capacity: 2762 cc
Valves: Inclined overhead with two ohcs per bank
Induction: Centrifugal supercharger
Wheelbase: 8 ft 4 in

Forward Speeds: 4
Front Suspension: Independent by lower wishbone, upper rocker arm and coil spring
Rear Suspension: Independent by transverse links, wishbone and coil spring
Chassis Frame: Tubular space-frame
Maximum Speed: 190 mph

Bobby Unser poses in the Novi-Ferguson called the STP-Oil Treatment Special after qualifying at 157.467 mph for the 1965 Indianopolis 500

Novi-Special America

The Novi was almost an institution at Indianapolis, for whereas most people opted for the 4·2-litre Offenhauser unblown engine during the 1950s, the Novi had its own engine, designed and developed by Jean Marcenac. It was a 3-litre V8 with a centrifugal supercharger, and was undoubtedly the most powerful racing car to compete at Indy in its day. Success seldom came its way, the engines tending to fly apart at critical moments, but when the Novi went it really went. The Novi engine, named after Route No. V1, where it was built, was used in front-wheel-drive, rear-wheel-drive and 4-wheel-drive Indianapolis variants over the years, and the rear-wheel-drive version ran at Monza in 1957 in the 500 Mile Race. It set a lap record on the banked track at 177·046 mph, reaching 190 mph on the straights.

Duke Nalon in the front-wheel-drive 3-litre supercharged V8 Novi Special at Indianapolis in 1948

Year: 1946/62
Model: Indianapolis
Engine: Novi
Number of cylinders: 8 in-vee
Bore and Stroke: 80·2 × 66·7 mm
Capacity: 2762 cc
Valves: Inclined overhead with two camshafts per bank
Induction: Centrifugal supercharger

Wheelbase: 8 ft 0 in
Forward Speeds: 2
Front Suspension: Rigid beam axle on torsion bars
Rear Suspension: Rigid axle on torsion bars
Chassis Frame: Tubular
Maximum Speed: 190 mph

OBM Anglo–German

Like the German AFM and Veritas firms, certain English racing drivers also used the pre-war 328 BMW sports car as the basis for a single-seater racing car for the post-war 'voiturette' racing that became Formula 2 in 1948. One

Osca Moore about to test his newly finished single-seater OBM in 1949

of these was Oscar B. Moore, a London motor trader, who took the 328 BMW GHX 516, and converted it into a single-seater and called it the OBM. The engine was tuned to run on an alcohol fuel, the driving seat and steering column moved nearer the centre-line of the chassis and magnesium alloy wheels fitted and a light-alloy body built. It was completed towards the end of 1948 and Moore took part in a great number of Continental road-races during 1949, preferring natural road circuits to the British aerodrome racing of that time.

Year: 1949
Model: Formula 2
Engine: 328 BMW
Number of cylinders: 6
Bore and Stroke: 66 × 96 mm
Capacity: 1971 cc
Valves: Inclined overhead with cross-pushrods
Induction: Three down-draught carburettors

Wheelbase: 7 ft 10½ in
Forward Speeds: 4
Front Suspension: Independent by transverse leaf spring and wishbones
Rear Suspension: Semi-elliptic leaf springs
Chassis Frame: Tubular
Maximum Speed: 130 mph

Osca

Italy

The Maserati brothers, Ernesto and Bindo, left the Maserati Company to the Orsi family in 1947, and started a new firm in Bologna entitled Officine Specializate Costruzione Automobili Fratelli Maserati, or OSCA Maserati for short, this ultimately being reduced to Osca. They made 1100-cc sports cars, which were then popular in Italian racing. Soom afterwards they built a 4½-litre V12-cylinder unsupercharged engine that would fit into the 4CLT/48 chassis, which was destined for the current Formula 1, and Prince Bira had one installed in his Maserati chassis in 1951. It had a bore and stroke of 78 × 78 mm and developed nearly 300 bhp, but this was insufficient to cope with the rising unblown Ferraris. Interest was turning to smaller 2-litre cars, and at the end of 1951 a complete new Osca 4½-litre car appeared briefly at Monza for the Italian GP, but it was already outdated.

The Maserati brothers built two 6-cylinder 2-litre cars, that were scaled-down versions of the 4½-litre car, and these participated in racing during 1952/3, driven by Louis Chiron and Elie Bayol.

Osca took no part in the 1954/60 GP racing, concentrating on sports cars which were more saleable, but with the introduction of Formula Junior they built one of the prettiest little front-engined cars, powered by a Fiat 1100-cc engine which had been worked on by themselves. In 1959 they had shown signs of being interested in the then Formula 2, having a very powerful 1½-litre sports-car engine with desmodromic valve gear. They got as far as making two chassis frames for these new single-seaters, but they were never completed.

Their main interest has always been engines, and Osca engines either 4- or 6-cylinder twin ohc units, have always been noted for their smoothness and cleanliness. Some 1½-litre 4-cylinder engines were sold to Alessandro de Tomaso who used them in his de Tomaso racing cars, while another Osca engine project was the development of the twin-cam 4-cylinder 1½-litre for mass production for Fiat to put into a road-going sports car.

Although the Orsi family continued the name Maserati the real line of Maserati engineering was continued by Osca, for these cars carried the unmistakable stamp of the instinctive genius of the Maserati brothers. The ex-Bira 4½-litre V12-engined car had a chequered career after he sold it, spending a long time in Australia and then returning to the UK where it was hacked around in Club racing. It was then taken into the Donington Park Racing Car Museum and returned to as-new condition and can be seen alongside a conventional 4CLT/48 Maserati. The 1951 car that Franco Rol drove at Monza, was turned into a sports car and resides in a French museum, and a similar fate befell Chiron's 2-litre Formula 2 Osca. The other Formula 2 car is still in original condition, owned by a member of the VSCC.

left Elie Bayol's Formula 2 OSCA on the occasion of its first appearance, at the Comminges GP in 1952

right Mario Andretti in action with the Parnelli VPJ4 in the 1975 British GP at Silverstone

Year: 1952
Model: Formula 2
Engine: Osca
Number of cylinders: 6
Bore and Stroke: 76 × 73 mm
Capacity: 1987 cc
Valves: Inclined overhead with two ohcs
Induction: Three double-choke Weber carburettors

Wheelbase: 7 ft 4½ in
Forward Speeds: 4
Front Suspension: Independent by double wishbones and coil springs
Rear Suspension: de Dion with quarter-elliptic leaf springs
Chassis Frame: Tubular
Maximum Speed: 145 mph

Parnelli

Anglo–American

The 1963 Indianapolis winner, Rufus Parnelli Jones has long been involved in things mechanical with the accent on motor racing. With his business partner in American racing, Velco Miletich, he decided to join in Formula 1 racing as a constructor, having already built his own cars for USAC racing after retiring from competition driving and running teams in almost every American branch of motor sport. He had engaged Maurice Phillippe, an ex-Lotus designer, to draw up the USAC cars, so the VPJ4 was a logical progression from them, using all the best British Formula 1 bits and pieces, such as Cosworth DFV engine, Hewland gearbox, Girling brakes. Phillippe left Lotus at the height of the success of the Lotus 72 in which he had played a big part, so it was no surprise that the Parnelli cars resembled the Lotus cars and that the new Formula 1 VPJ4 resembled an uprated Lotus 72. The debut of the new car was in the Canadian GP of 1974 driven by Mario Andretti, when it finished 7th. In the following race at Watkins Glen for the USA GP it qualified third fastest in practice.

In 1975 the team set up a base in Norfolk, not far from the Lotus factory, and actually lured some of the Lotus mechanics away to work for them. With Mario Andretti still driving, the Vel's-Parnelli Formula 1 car took to the

world's circuits. Parnelli himself did not appear at the European races and the team seemed to lack direction or purpose, with no one very obviously in charge of development. It was never anything more than an also-ran and only lasted through 1975 and the early part of 1976 before it quietly faded away. The Parnelli Jones empire continued to be active in American racing but the Formula 1 efforts are best forgotten.

Year: 1975	*Forward Speeds:* 5 Hewland
Model: VPJ4	*Front Suspension:* Independent by
Engine: Cosworth DFV	wishbones and torsion bars
Number of cylinders: 8 in-vee	*Rear Suspension:* Independent by
Bore and Stroke: 85·6 × 64·8 mm	transverse links, radius rods, and
Capacity: 2993 cc	torsion bars
Valves: 4 per cylinder two ohcs	*Chassis Frame:* Aluminium
per bank	monocoque; engine a stressed
Induction: Lucas fuel-injection	member
Wheelbase: 8 ft 4 in	*Maximum Speed:* 175 mph

Penske   Anglo–American

American businessman Roger Penske ran teams in various forms of racing throughout the USA with every success and spread an aura of omnipotence among the mass media, so that when he said he would be tackling the Formula 1 scene in full in 1975 there was great interest among the European teams. His new car had already made a brief appearance in the North American races at the end of 1974. One thing that Penske Racing had never skimped on was an immaculate turn-out for men and machines and with money not being in short supply, they brought a glitter to Formula 1 with their conventionally designed Penske PC 1 powered by a Cosworth DFV engine.

Although the sources of money and inspiration came from America most of the know-how and work came from England, with Englishman Geoffrey Ferris doing the design work and with English mechanics and English firms building the car. Roger Penske's long-standing friend and driver Mark Donohue, came out of brief retirement to drive the car but throughout 1975 they did not seem to be making much headway.

Half-way through the season they began to despair of keeping up with the opposition and bought a March 751 for comparative research against their own car. At the Austrian GP in August Penske received a severe blow, for during practice a front tyre deflated on the March 751 and Donohue left the track at high speed and subsequently died from his injuries. After a moment of darkness, Penske was back in action again with Ulsterman John Watson driving a new car. This was the Penske PC3 and it was very March-like in its design and construction.

In 1976 Watson continued to drive for Penske Racing with the PC3 until an entirely new car, the PC4, was ready. With this new car the team progressed noticeably and became much more competitive until Watson won their first victory, ironically, at the Austrian GP where 12 months before they had suffered so much grief. That was their zenith, for though the car went well for the reat of the season it did not win again and by November after disagreements with his major sponsor, Penske was forced to withdraw the whole operation from its Dorsetshire headquarters and return to America. The two PC4 cars were bought by the German ATS wheel company and raced throughout 1977 as ATS-Penske cars. They formed the basis for a new ATS design of Formula 1 car.

Year: 1976
Model: PC4
Engine: Cosworth DFV
Number of Cylinders: 8 in-vee
Bore and Stroke: 85·6 × 64·8 mm
Capacity: 2993 cc
Valves: 4 per cylinder, two ohcs per bank
Induction: Lucas fuel injection
Wheelbase: 9 ft 0¼ in
Forward Speeds: 5 Hewland
Front Suspension: Independent, double wishbones, inboard coil spring
Rear Suspension: Independent, single transverse top link, twin lower links, double radius rods and coil springs

Chassis Frame: Aluminium monocoque; engine a stressed member
Maximum Speed: 180 mph

Ulsterman John Watson in the Penske PC4 on its first public appearance

Porsche   Germany

The Austrian Dr. Ferdinand Porsche, who was a pupil of Prof. Rumpler, was one of the leading designers in pre-war Germany, working for Austro-Daimler, Steyr, Benz and Daimler-Benz. In the 1930s Porsche set up as a consulting engineer and became the leader of the Auto Union design team. After the 1939–45 war his son Ferry carried on the consulting firm, and soon developed a sports car out of his father's Volkswagen design, the Porsche sports car making a name for itself in competitions and being produced in great numbers over the years.

In 1952 the firm designed a new racing engine, of flat 4-cylinder layout and air-cooled, but having twin ohcs to each pair of cylinders. This very powerful 1500-cc engine was developed through sports-car racing, and as the firm became financially stronger, due to increased sales of production Porches, they were able to turn their thoughts to GP racing. Starting by making one of their sports cars into a single-seater, which was facilitated by the engine being at the back, they later rejected the fully enveloping sports body and built a car with a GP single-seater body. In 1960 they took part in Formula 2 racing with a team of single-seater cars, and continued in 1961 with the new 1½-litre Formula. The 4-cylinder engine having reached the limit of its development, they built a new horizontally opposed 8-cylinder unit, still air-cooled and naturally mounted behind the driver, as these two concepts of design had always been advocated by Dr. Porsche. Teething troubles delayed the appearance of the new engines, but a new chassis was tried out in 1961. Porsche had designed a system of i.f.s. that used two trailing links to each wheel and transversely mounted torsion bars, one great merit of this layout being that the wheel track did not vary with wheel movement, thereby making steering geometry simpler. The new chassis departed from the age-old Porsche design by having wishbone and coil-spring front suspension. Rear suspension on the racing cars began with swing axles, on the same principle as the Auto Union and Volkswagen, and was later changed to a system of double wishbones of unequal length, operating in different planes. Thus the wheel movement was predetermined rather than being the outcome of suspension movement, as is the case with many double wishbone designs. In 1962 another new chassis was designed with double wishbones and torsion bars all round and this was adopted for the 8-cylinder cars.

An outstanding feature of all Porsche designs has been the gearbox, their system of baulk-ring syncromesh being unique and used by many other manufacturers. On the racing Porsches in 1962 the gearbox had six speeds in order to deal with the 10,000 rpm of the 8-cylinder engine.

Finding that the opposition in Formula 1 was stiffer than expected, and being unable to dominate the scene, the Porsche factory withdrew from GP racing in 1963 and concentrated on sports-car and GT racing, which they still do to this day, being the leaders in technical development in long-distance

left Hans Herrmann rounding the Karussel at the Nurburgring in 1960 in a 4-cylinder Formula 2 Porsche

right Dan Gurney in a flat-8-cylinder Formula 1 Porsche in 1962

racing. They never returned to single-seater racing and it is unlikely that they ever will, for they view the scene today as lacking in any possibility of providing technical development, so restrict their racing activities to sports-cars and GT racing.

Year: 1960
Model: F2 Type 718
Engine: Porsche (air-cooled)
Number of cylinders: 4 horizontally-opposed
Bore and Stroke: 85 × 66 mm
Capacity: 1498 cc
Valves: Inclined overhead with two camshafts per bank
Induction: Down-draught carburettors
Wheelbase: 7 ft 2½ in
Forward Speeds: 6
Front Suspension: Independent by trailing arms and torsion bars
Rear Suspension: Independent by wishbones and coil springs
Chassis Frame: Tubular space-frame
Maximum Speed: 150 mph

Year: 1962
Model: F1 Type 804
Engine: Porsche (air-cooled)
Number of cylinders: 8 horizontally-opposed
Bore and Stroke: 66 × 54·5 mm
Capacity: 1492 cc
Valves: Inclined overhead with two camshafts per bank
Induction: Down-draught carburettors
Wheelbase: 7 ft 6½ in
Forward Speeds: 6
Front and Rear Suspension: Independent by double wishbones and torsion bars
Chassis Frame: Tubular space-frame
Maximum Speed: 160 mph

Railton-Mobil Special   England

Long-time holder of the World's Flying Mile Record in the unlimited category, or the Land Speed Record as it is popularly known, was John Cobb with the twin-engined Railton car. This was designed by Reid Railton and built by

Thomson & Taylor Ltd. in 1938. Cobb set new records in 1938 and 1939. After the war he returned to the Bonneville Salt Flats in 1947, backed by the Mobil Oil Company, and set the record to 394·196 mph with a best one-way run of 403·135 mph.

When the car was designed it broke fresh ground in that it used 4-wheel-drive, independent front suspension, a backbone chassis frame and weighed a mere 3 tons 2½ cwt, for at the time other contenders were building cars that weighed as much as 7 tons. Railton's theory was to keep the weight down and use 4-wheel-drive for maximum acceleration, for the 6-mile run-in at Bonneville was proving the limitation for attaining 400 mph.

The box-section backbone chassis was in the form of a shallow S, with a Napier Lion 12-cylinder broad-arrow aero-engine mounted in each surve of the S, one driving the front wheels and the other the rear, each with its own 3-speed gearbox, while the driver sat out ahead of the front wheels. One of the most perfect aerodynamic bodies was built and by using a 75-gallon ice-tank for the engine-cooling there was no loss by drag through radiators.

After Cobb's death in 1952 while attempting the Water Speed Record, the car was kept by the Mobil company as a museum piece and can still be seen in the Birmingham Science Museum. As a piece of outstanding design work it is a landmark in record-breaking history and to this day is a tribute to the genius of Reid Railton. There is little doubt that its full potential was never exploited.

John Cobb at speed on the Bonneville Salt Flats in 1947 in the Railton Mobil Special

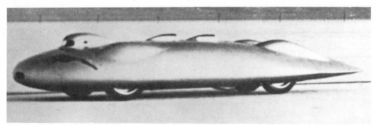

Year: 1938
Model: Record
Engines: Napier Lion
Number of cylinders: 12 each engine
Bore and Stroke: 139·7 × 130·2 mm
Capacity: 23,970 cc
Valves: Overhead with ohc to each bank
Induction: Centrifugal supercharger

Wheelbase: 13 ft 6 in
Forward Speeds: 3
Front Suspension: Independent by wishbones and coil springs
Rear Suspension: Rigid axle on coil springs
Chassis Frame: Box-section backbone
Maximum Speed: 400 mph

162

Ralt Australia

When Jack Brabham gave up racing and racing-car manufacture, to return home to Australia in 1970, his partner Ron Tauranac who did all the design work, stayed on with the new owner of Brabham's firm. It was not long before there came a parting of the ways and Tauranac left the firm he had helped to start. After a time as a racing-car consultant designer, helping with numerous Formula 1 projects, Ron decided to go back into racing-car manufacture and started back at square one, building a simple tubular space-frame chassis for Formula Ford and then adapting it for F3, soon moving on into Formula

A 1976 Ralt RT1 Formula 3 in action

2 with the same basic design. With his background and personal interest in the car it was not surprising that there were plenty of customers from all countries. Like the Brabham cars he had marketed, the Ralts sold by their successes. The Formula 3 Tauranac cars, powered mostly by the Japanese Toyota engine tuned by the Italian Novamotor firm, were soon a strong force in International events during 1976, and 70 cars were built by the start of 1977.

In 1977 they proved particularly successful in Formula 2, while the lower Formulae continued to see Ralt cars to the fore. It was a Ralt that achieved the first victory for the V6 Ferrari engine in Formula 2 in 1977, a side-activity that the Maranello firm have been toying with. Hill-climbs and sprint events have also seen Ralt cars in use and among the small racing-car constructors Ron Tauranac has established himself once more as a man who can deliver the goods for the private owner.

Before coming to England to join Jack Brabham's racing-car firm, Tauranac had built racing-car specials in Australia and they were known then as Ralt, a name derived from his and his brother's initials, Ron and Austin Lewis Tauranac, so he revived the name for his new cars, which are really more in the Brabham Tauranac (BT) tradition than are the current Brabham racing cars.

Year: 1976
Model: RT1 Formula 3
Engine: Toyota
Number of cylinders: 4
Bore and Stroke: 87 × 84 mm
Capacity: 1996 cc
Valves: Inclined overhead with two ohcs
Induction: Fuel injection

Wheelbase: 8 ft 0¼ in
Forward Speeds: 5 Hewland
Front Suspension: Wishbones and coil springs
Rear Suspension: Transverse links, radius rods and coil springs
Chassis Frame: Tubular space-frame
Maximum Speed: 145 mph

Renault

France

The Regie-Renault empire has been involved in all forms of motor sport for a long time, mostly through subsidiaries like Alpine, and has supported activities as widespread as rallies and Formula 3. They developed turbo-charging on their competition V6 engine in sports-car racing and in 1977 entered the very specialized field of Formula 1 through a direct subsidiary, Renault-Sport. The Renault made a radical break-away in Formula 1 by adopting the turbo-charged 1½-litre engine against the unsupercharged 3-litres of the rest of the world.

The RS01 Renault was the first single-seater pure GP car to come from Regie-Renault and proved to be a small and compact car built along current Formula 1 chassis lines. The 90-degree V6 engine drives through a 6-speed Hewland gearbox and the exhaust-driven turbo-charger is mounted above the clutch housing; it feeds compressed air forwards across the engine to an inter-cooler behind the cockpit and then backwards to the inlet manifold. Petrol is fed into the inlet ports by high-pressure injection and the engine is cooled by water radiators on each side of the engine bay.

The works driver for 1977 was Jean-Pierre Jabouille, long associated with Renault sporting projects, and while the initial season did not afford any success to the new car it showed real potential and ran strongly in the mid-field of the very competitive Formula 1 scene. Engine reliability was not a strong point, while problems arose with the exhaust-driven turbine and the compressor, but such teething troubles on a potential 500 bhp power unit of only 1½ litres were to be expected. The Renault RS01, even with its comparatively inexperienced driver caused a lot of other teams to keep a very close watch on its progress throughout 1977.

Year: 1977
Model: RS 01—Formula 1
Engine: Renault-Gordini
Number of cylinders: 6 in-vee
Bore and Stroke: 86 × 42·8 mm
Capacity: 1492 cc
Valves: 4 per cylinder, two ohcs per bank
Induction: Exhaust driven turbocharger
Wheelbase: 8 ft 2½ in (2500 mm)

Forward Speeds: 6 Hewland
Front Suspension: Double wishbone layout with inboard coil springs
Rear Suspension: Twin lower links, single upper link, double radius rods, coil springs
Chassis Frame: Aluminium monocoque; engine a stressed member
Maximum Speed: 190 mph

Riley   England

The Riley Company dates back to 1896, but it was not until the Vintage years that they showed any interest in competitions. The first sporting Riley was the side-valve Redwing model and in 1926 the 'Nine' was introduced. This advanced 4-cylinder engine had inclined overhead valves and hemispherical

left The Renault RS01 Formula 1 car on its debut to the Press in Paris

right Percy Maclure winning the 1938 International Trophy race at Brooklands in his Riley with i.f.s. and 1.7-litre 6-cylinder engine

combustion chambers, as well as individual inlet and exhaust ports to each cylinder. Parry Thomas and Reid Railton combined to produce a very low slung sports/racing version of the 1100-cc 4-cylinder, and in 1929 the Riley Company put it into production, calling it the 'Brooklands' model. The engine responded to almost endless tuning, though the two-bearing crankshaft was the final limiting factor.

The 'Brooklands' model was built for competitions, having good road-holding and brakes, and a very fine close-ratio 4-speed gearbox. The Riley Company produced special parts for it to enable customers to race them successfully. Among those to build racing versions of this sports car were F.W. Dixon, whose track-racing Riley Nine lapped Brooklands at 113 mph, and A.F. Ashby, whose long-tailed car won the 1932 Duke of York's Trophy race at 102·69 mph.

Meanwhile the Riley firm produced a 1½-litre 6-cylinder touring car with the same style of engine, which in production form was very sluggish. However, this formed the basis for some very fast racing Rileys, of both 1½ and 2 litres, the parent firm making special cylinder heads, cranks, rods etc., to convert these 6-cylinder engines into racing units. Notable among these was the Raymond Mays' 'White Riley', which was supercharged and became the prototype of the ERA. Dixon produced some remarkably fast 6-cylinder 2-litre Rileys, noted for their light polished aluminium bodies. The Riley Company were concentrating on sports-car racing at the time (the Ulter TT in particular), so that engine development and tuning was continuous at the factory and benefitted the racing customers.

In 1936 the company built some single-seater cars for sale, with i.f.s. by a rather clumsy system of swing axles and coil springs, known as the Andre-Girling system, and orthodox rear axles on semi-elliptic leaf springs. Two alternative engines were offered, a 4-cylinder of 1½ litres, or a 6-cylinder 2-litre, with a single Amal carburettor to each cylinder; the well-tried Riley 'crash' gearbox was used with torque-tube final drive. The cars had bulbous radiator cowlings and long tails with head fairing, while the steering was offset so that the driver sat alongside the torque tube, a petrol tank filling the passenger side of this narrow car. Coming at a time when the ERA was very popular and successful, the single-seater Riley did not catch on, being heavier and less powerful than the ERA.

One of the staunchest supporters of Rileys up to 1939 was Percy Maclure, who did remarkably well in British handicap racing with his 6-cylinder car, in various forms depending on the handicap arrangements. He had 1100-cc 1½-litre, 1·7-litre and 2-litre engines available. With the introduction of the 1½-litre 4-cylinder 'Sprite' sports car, some of these chassis were used to build racing versions, such as those used by F.R. Gerard and J.F. Gee. When Nuffield took over the Riley factory all racing activity and development ceased, but the cars were raced on by private owners.

In the immediate post-war period of British racing many of the pre-war Rileys were rejuvenated and did well in the hands of such drivers as Fairman, Harrison and Hawthorn. Today in VSCC racing the Riley Nine still forms the basis of numerous racing specials.

Year: 1936	*Wheelbase:* 8 ft 3 in
Model: Single-seater	*Forward Speeds:* 4
Engine: Riley	*Front Suspension:* Independent by
Number of cylinders: 4 or 6	transverse links, radius arms and
Bore and Stroke: 69 × 100 mm or	coil springs
63·5 × 104·5 mm	*Rear Suspension:* Semi-elliptic leaf
Capacity: 1496 cc or 1986 cc	springs
Valves: Inclined overhead with	*Chassis Frame:* Box-section
pushrods	*Maximum Speed:* 130 mph in
Induction: Multiple carburettors	2-litre form

Rover England

The Rover Company produced cars as long ago as 1904, and in 1907 one of them won the Tourist Trophy, but apart from this the firm showed no inclination towards serious racing. However, they produced sporting cars which featured in amateur competitions throughout the Vintage years and in the '30s. In 1948 Peter Wilks, George Mackay and Spencer King of the Rover experimental department built a single-seater car from production Rover parts, and in 1949/50 they raced it in British meetings and in hill-climbs. Started as a spare-time hobby, it later received the company blessing and underwent a lot of development, providing much useful information for the technical department, especially on suspension and roadholding matters.

Today the car is very active in Historic racing, running with a later 3-litre Rover engine installed in place of the special 6-cylinder 2-litre unit.

Spencer King in the single-seater Rover in 1949

Year: 1948/51
Model: F2
Engine: Rover
Bore and Stroke: 63·5 × 105 mm
Capacity: 1996 cc
Valves: Overhead inlet, side exhaust
Induction: Three SU carburettors

Wheelbase: 7 ft 9 in
Forward Speeds: 4
Front Suspension: Independent by wishbones and coil springs
Rear Suspension: de Dion with quarter-elliptic leaf springs
Chassis Frame: Box-section
Maximum Speed: 115 mph

RRA
England

Built by Geoff Richardson, the original RRA began life as the Percy Maclure Riley, with Andre-Girling i.f.s. and ERA engine replacing the 6-cylinder Riley engine. Richardson acquired the car in 1948, fitted a new body and raced it that year. For 1949 he had a new chassis frame made, removed the i.f.s., engine and gearbox from the Maclure car and created the Richardson Racing Automobile as a single-seater with i.r.s. by swing axles. The car was developed and raced by him until 1955, the engine being enlarged to 2 litres. Subsequently the engine was sold to an ERA owner and the rest of the car sold elsewhere.

A second RRA was built in 1955, using the chassis of the single-seater Aston Martin built by the works for Tasman Racing. A special 2·4-litre Jaguar engine replaced the Aston engine, the suspension and brakes were altered and the RRA-Jaguar came into being. At the end of its racing career it was converted into a road car, with all-enveloping body. In 1960 Richardson built his third RRA, utilizing a Formula 1 Cooper chassis, into which he installed a 2½-litre Connaught/Alta engine. When he sold the car at the end of season the Connaught engine was replaced by a Buick V8.

Year: 1949
Model: F1
Engine: ERA
Number of cylinders: 6
Bore and Stroke: 57·5 × 95·2 mm
Capacity: 1488 cc
Valves: Inclined overhead operated by pushrods
Induction: Supercharged

Wheelbase: 8 ft 3 in
Forward Speeds: 4 (Riley)
Front Suspension: Independent by transverse links, radius arms and coil springs
Rear Suspension: Independent by swing axles
Chassis Frame: Box-section
Maximum Speed: 135 mph

Sacha-Gordine France

This car is a member of the small but select band of costly GP projects that never reached the racing circuit. Inspired by Monsieur Sacha-Gordine, a French film producer, and designed by Monsieur Vigna, a student of Dr. Porsche, the car had much in common with the ill-fated Cisitalia. Started in 1952, the design was very advanced, with a V8-cylinder engine behind the driver, coupled directly to a 5-speed gearbox, the tubular chassis having Porsche-type i.f.s. by torsion bars, and de Dion rear axle also on torsion bars. One car was nearly completed early in 1953, but then the money ran out and the project was abandoned, which was not surprising as nearly every casting on the car was in expensive magnesium alloy. Sacha-Gordine continued to be as successful in the film industry as he was unsuccessful in building a GP car.

below left Geoff Richardson in the rebuilt Maclure Riley in single-seater RRA form at Silverstone in 1953
below The nearest the Sacha-Gordine ever got to running was when it was wheeled out of the factory for photographic and publicity purposes in 1952

Year: 1952
Model: Formula 2
Engine: Sacha-Gordine
Number of cylinders: 8 in-vee
Bore and Stroke: 70 × 64 mm
Capacity: 1970 cc
Valves: Inclined overhead with
two ohcs per bank
Induction: Four carburettors

Wheelbase: 8 ft 5½ in
Forward Speeds: 5
Front Suspension: Independent by
trailing arms and transverse torsion
bars
Rear Suspension: de Dion with
torsion bars
Chassis Frame: Tubular
Maximum Speed: Unknown

Scarab

America

The name Scarab was given to sports cars built by Lance Reventlow and his
associates in 1957. These were very successful in American amateur racing,
as they were built and designed on a foundation of knowledge gained when
Reventlow and Warren Olsen visited Europe.

As Reventlow was the son of millionairess Barbara Hutton, there was
ample money available, and they embarked on the building of a Formula 1
GP car for 1959, designing and making everything themselves, including the
engine. The design followed many trends started by European firms; the chassis
frame was of small-diameter tubing as on Lotus or Cooper, while the engine
owed much to Mercedes-Benz, being laid on its side and having desmodromic
valve gear, though it was only a 4-cylinder.

Development work on the engine and gearbox took much longer than
anticipated, and the car was not ready to race until the beginning of the 1960
season. Reventlow and Chuck Daigh competed at a number of European GP
races, but were hopelessly outclassed, for design had progressed enormously
in the previous twelve months and the rear-engined revolution had arrived.
Before half the season was completed the Scarabs were packed up and sent
back to California and work was started on new cars.

left The short-lived Scarab GP car
during the 1960 Belgian GP at
Francorchamps

right The SEFAC behind the pits at
Reims during practice for the French
GP of 1938

They failed to make their mark due to the delay caused by the development of the engine, its advanced specification being rather more than the knowledge and facilities of Reventlow and his associates could deal with. In 1961 they made another attempt, with a 3-litre engine for Inter-Continental Formula, but this was doomed to failure, and once more too late, they built a rear-engined car with a Buick V8 engine for Inter-Continental in 1962, failing to see that the Formula was dying rapidly. Before the 1962 season started Reventlow decided to cut his losses and close down his factory before he made any more expensive 'too-late' attempts. Still a young man, Lance Reventlow was tragically killed in a private-aircraft accident in 1973.

Year: 1960
Model: Formula 1
Engine: Scarab
Number of cylinders: 4
Bore and Stroke: 95·25 × 85·73 mm
Capacity: 2441 cc
Valves: Inclined overhead with two ohcs and 'desmodromic' operation

Induction: Hilborn fuel-injection
Wheelbase: 7 ft 6 in
Forward Speeds: 4
Front and Rear Suspension: Independent by double wishbones and coil springs
Chassis Frame: Tubular space-frame
Maximum Speed: 155 mph

SEFAC France

A designer of early Salmsons, Emile Petit, formed a company in the 1930s known as the *Société des Etudes et de Fabrication d'Automobile de Course,* or in other words a company for the study and building of racing cars. The initials SEFAC were used and the object was to produce a GP car for the 1934 Formula of 750 kg. One SEFAC was built, an 8-cylinder 2·8-litre which appeared briefly for the French GP of 1935 and once or twice the following year, but it was never ready to race and was always withdrawn after practice.

It was still eligible for the 1938/39 Formula of 3-litres supercharged, and in 1938 actually started in a race, the French GP at Reims. It lasted only a lap! Its last appearance was at Pau in 1939.

The car was unusual in that the engine was built like two 4-cylinders with twin ohc, mounted side-by-side on a common crankcase, geared together at the rear of the crankshafts and so running in opposite directions. The right-hand crank drove a huge supercharger and the left-hand one the 4-speed ENV-Wilson pre-selector gearbox. It had i.f.s. and a rigid rear axle, the body had an offset driving position and the steering had a drag link to each front wheel, joined by an inverted T-shaped member that was rotated by the steering column worm.

In 1948 Emile Petit made another attempt to launch this car, forming a company called Dommartin, and he threatened to bring out the renamed SEFAC, now running without the supercharger and having been enlarged to 3619 cc by increasing the bore from 70 to 80 mm. The Dommartin was no more successful than the SEFAC; in fact, less so, for it never raced at all.

Year: 1934
Model: Grand Prix
Engine: Petit design
Number of cylinders: 8 in two rows of four
Bore and Stroke: 70 × 90 mm
Capacity: 2760 cc
Valves: Inclined overhead with four ohcs
Induction: Two carburettors and

Petit vane-type supercharger
Wheelbase: 8 ft 10¼ in (2700 mm)
Forward Speeds: 4
Front Suspension: Independent by forward facing links and coil springs
Rear Suspension: Rigid axle on coil springs
Chassis Frame: Channel-section
Maximum Speed: Unknown

Shadow
Anglo–American

The Shadow car is the product of Don Nichols' Advanced Vehicle Systems (AVS), a company who built cars for American racing before embarking on a European Formula 1 programme. With large financial backing from the Universal Oil Products (UOP) Company of Illinois, the UOP-Shadow was launched on the scene in 1973. Designed by Tony Southgate, who had worked for Lola, Brabham, Dan Gurney's Eagle firm and then BRM, the DN1 series got the team off to a good start, the all-black cars powered by Cosworth DFV engines, making a promising showing during the season. The Formula 1 cars were mostly odd-numbers in the DN series, DN3, DN5 etc, while even numbers were for cars in the American racing programme which was running concurrently with the European programme. The firm was based at Northampton, very near the Cosworth engine factory, and until 1976 was among the front-runners. In 1975 they flirted with the idea of

Tom Pryce, who won the non-Championship Race of Champions for Shadow is seen in a 1975 DN5. He was killed in an accident in the 1977 S.A. GP

using the French Matra V12 engine, and a single DN7 was built, but the project foundered, despite the best efforts of Jean-Pierre Jarier. Some of the earlier cars were sold into private hands for use in club racing.

When UOP pulled out at the end of 1975 and Southgate left to join the Lotus team. Nichols continued on his own, but limited finances hampered the team, especially with regard to development and new cars, and the DN8 was very late in being completed, David Wass taking over from Southgate. By this time the DN5 had been surpassed, lacking development time. Run as Shadow cars in 1976 and 1977, the team had to rely on numerous small sponsors. Success came in the latter year when Australian Alan Jones won the Austrian GP, the team's first major victory.

The DN2 and DN4 were sports cars for American Can–Am racing, and the DN6 a F5000 single-seater, used exclusively in American racing, run by the USA branch of AVS. The team had a major set-back at the beginning of 1974 when Peter Revson was killed when suspension failure caused a crash in the new DN3 while testing at the Kyalami circuit in South Africa.

Year: 1975
Model: DN5
Engine: Cosworth DFV
Number of cylinders: 8 in-vee
Bore and Stroke: 85·6 × 64·8 mm
Capacity: 2993 cc
Valves: 4 per cylinder, two ohcs per bank
Induction: Lucas fuel-injection
Wheelbase: 8 ft 9 in

Forward Speeds: 5 Hewland FL200
Front Suspension: Independent by double wishbones and coil springs
Rear Suspension: Independent by transverse link, wishbone, radius rods and coil springs
Chassis Frame: Aluminium monocoque; engine a stressed member
Maximum Speed: 175 mph

Squire

England

The Squire was a small-production, high-quality sports car built by Adrian Squire near Henley-on-Thames around 1935–36, each car being individually hand-made. The chassis was very low-slung, with wide track and used a 1½-litre twin-ohc Anzani engine, with a Roots supercharger. This drove through a Wilson pre-selector gearbox to an underslung rear axle. Only a handful of these cars was built, but each one was given a certificate to show that it had lapped Brooklands track at over 100 mph.

Apart from being costly, the Squire was one of the fastest sports cars of the day and this prompted the firm to build a single-seater version on the sports-car chassis. It raced at Brooklands in 1935 driven by Luis Fontes but was not fast enough to combat ERA and Alta opposition. It retired in the British Empire Trophy Race when the engine blew up and again in the 500 Mile Race when the chassis broke. It ran once more at Brooklands, gaining 3rd place in a Mountain circuit handicap event, but was then turned into a two-seater sports-bodied road car.

Year: 1935
Model: Single-seater
Engine: Anzani R1
Number of cylinders: 4
Bore and Stroke: 69 × 100 mm
Capacity: 1496 cc
Valves: Inclined overhead with two ohcs

Induction: Supercharged
Wheelbase: 8 ft 6 in
Forward Speeds: 4 ENV preselector
Front and Rear Suspension: Semi-elliptic leaf springs
Chassis Frame: Channel-section
Maximum Speed: 125 mph

left Luis Fontes driving the single-seater Squire during the British Empire Trophy at Brooklands in 1935

below right R. Parnelli-Jones in the STP-Turbocar after qualifying 6th fastest at 166.075 mph for the 1967 Indianapolis 500

Stanguellini

Italy

Built by Vittorio Stanguellini in Modena since 1948, these cars began as modified Fiat sports cars, which he developed until he was making the complete car, with 750-cc twin-ohc engines. He built tiny single-seater racing cars, using these engines, for Italian National Formula 3. When Formula

Junior was mooted Stanguellini was the first to go into production and, being a Fiat agent, he once more used modified Fiat components. His early front-engined cars were most successful in 1959 and still did quite well the following year when Formula Junior became International. He finally had to follow the English lead and build rear-engined Juniors but these had little success. His work on tuning Fiats, as well as providing tune-up kits for production Fiats, is well known.

A Formula Junior Stanguellini at the pits at Monza in 1959. Truly a mini-GP car

Year: 1959
Model: Formula Junior
Engine: Fiat
Number of cylinders: 4
Bore and Stroke: 68 × 75 mm
Capacity: 1089 cc
Valves: Pushrod operated overhead
Induction: Two double-choke Weber carburettors

Wheelbase:
Forward Speeds: 4
Front Suspension: Independent with upper transverse leaf spring and lower wishbones
Rear Suspension: Rigid axle on coil springs
Chassis Frame: Tubular
Maximum Speed: 110 mph

STP-Turbocar   America

The Granatelli brothers, Andy, Vince and Joe, rocked the Indianapolis racing world in 1967 when they built a 4-wheel-drive car for the 500 Mile Race, powered by a Pratt & Whitney gas turbine engine. Named the STP-

Turbocar, and built in the STP-Paxton workshops, one of the many subsidiaries of the STP Corporation, the aircraft power plant was mounted on the left of the chassis, with the driver on the right. Without the need for cooling orifices for radiators the Turbocar presented a very smooth shape, with a sunken duct on the nose to take air to the turbine; the exhaust was on the top of the body by the left rear wheel.

Driven by Parnelli-Jones the Turbocar led until four laps from the end when a small bearing broke up and caused retirement. It was so quiet that tyre noise was the main sound to be heard while the Turbocar was running and many people opposed this 'quiet revolution', feeling the noise had to be part of motor racing. More serious to the Indianapolis establishment was the performance of the Turbocar and this aspect was dealt with by severe restrictions on the air intake size for turbine engines, thus curtailing the power. The Turbocar really made its mark on USAC racing, so much so that within a few years 4-wheel-drive and turbine engines were outlawed from American racing in order to protect the vested interests of those people concerned with the conventional piston engine. The original Turbocar only ran for one season, but was followed by the STP-Lotus 56 turbine-powered cars, until the rules put them out.

Year: 1967
Model: Indianapolis
Engine: Pratt & Witney turbine ST6B
Number of cylinders: none
Bore and Stroke: none
Capacity: Equivilence 4·2 litres
Valves: none
Induction: Fuel-injection

Wheelbase: 8 ft 0 in
Forward Speeds: none
Front Suspension: Independent, wishbones and coil springs
Rear Suspension: Independent, transverse links and coil springs
Chassis Frame: Fabricated steel structure
Maximum Speeds: 180 mph

Surtees   England

It was only natural for John Surtees to build his own racing cars, for all his life he was mechanically minded and had a hand in the building of Lola Formula 1 cars with his friend Eric Broadley. After a time with the Ferrari team and then Cooper, Honda and BRM he set out on his own, building Formula 5000 cars for sale. At first he could not support a racing team financially so concentrated on building single-seaters for sale, in F5000 and F2. In 1970 he raced a McLaren Formula 1 car and this soon led to the construction of his own car for GP racing, which was the TS7 and it appeared mid-season.

At the end of 1971 he retired from active driving and concentrated on building cars and running a team in Formula 1 and Formula 2, with backing from an outside sponsor. While his F1 cars were rather second-rate, the F2 cars were very good and Mike Hailwood won the European F2 Championship in 1972. After weathering financial and technical storms, which at times nearly caused the small Edenbridge factory to be closed down, John Surtees was rejuvinated in 1976 with strong sponsorship and while a GP victory still eludes his cars, he never fails to inspire his team to give of its best.

Following the lead set by the Lotus 49, using the Cosworth DFV engine and Hewland gearbox as the rear part of the car, cantilevered out behind the cockpit monocoque, Surtees follows his concept with simple and clean execution for his Formula 1 cars. The successful TS10 Formula 2 car used a 4-cylinder Ford engine and Hewland gearbox.

It can truly be said of John Surtees that he lives for racing and races for a living. Lacking very large finances he has never been able to attract a really top-flight driver into one of his cars, so that their true potential has never been demonatrated.

Year: 1972
Model: TS10 Formula 2
Engine: Ford BDA
Number of cylinders: 4
Bore and Stroke: 90·4 × 77·6 mm
Capacity: 1994 cc
Valves: Inclined overhead with twin ohcs
Induction: Lucas fuel-injection
Wheelbase: 7 ft 11 in

Forward Speeds: 5 Hewland FG400
Front Suspension: Independent by wishbones and coil springs
Rear Suspension: Independent by transverse link, wishbone and twin radius rods, coil springs
Chassis Frame: Aluminium monocoque
Maximum Speed: 160 mph

Year: 1976
Model: TS19 Formula 1
Engine: Cosworth DFV
Number of cylinders: 8 in-vee
Bore and Stroke: 85·6 × 64·8 mm
Capacity: 2993 cc
Valves: Four per cylinder, two ohcs per bank
Induction: Lucas fuel-injection
Wheelbase: 8 ft 2½ in
Forward Speeds: 5 Hewland
Front Suspension: Independent by double wishbones and coil springs
Rear Suspension: Independent by transverse link, wishbone, radius rods and coil springs

Chassis Frame: Aluminium monocoque; engine a stressed member
Maximum Speed: 180 mph

Australian Alan Jones driving a Surtees TS19 at the Nurburgring in the 1976 German GP

Talbot   England

The old Clement-Talbot firm joined the Sunbeam-Talbot-Darracq combine in 1920 and continued to build Talbot cars at Barlby Road in London. In 1925 Louis Coatalen, who was looking after the STD combine, installed Georges Roesch at the Talbot factory and he began a series of successful 6-cylinder cars, noted for their smoothness and silence, designed primarily as tourers. From these developed sporting versions, which were raced with success, and the Talbot agents, Fox & Nicholl Ltd., were soon running a team in the major races. For the 1930 Brooklands 500 Mile Race they built a special single-seater version of the sports '90' that performed extremely well and finished 4th at 104·26 mph. In 1931 the 3-litre '105' model was introduced and for the 500 Mile Race that year the Fox & Nicholl single-seater used one of these engines, and finished 2nd at 112·93 mph.

left The single-seater Talbot '90' on the Brooklands Banking during a 'mountain' race in 1930

right A Talbot-Lago being wheeled to the starting grid of the 1950 Spanish GP

Their long chassis and good suspension was very suited to track racing, and after the success of the Fox & Nicholl car others were built by Dr. Roth and G.A. Wooding, while W.M. Cooper used the works faired-in 4-seater bodied '110' model, which superseded the '105', being of 3·3 litres. They were regular Brooklands competitors, noted for their silent running and unobtrusive speed, Couper ultimately lapping at 129 mph with his car, without the need of such complications as two ohcs, superchargers or racing fuel. The pushrod vertical-valve layout of the Roesch design was unchanged from the inception of the 14/45 in 1925. When Rootes Brothers took over the Talbot firm in the mid-'30s all development work on the Roesch design finished and the Talbot disappeared.

Year: 1930/4
Model: Type 110
Engine: Talbot
Number of cylinders: 6
Bore and Stroke: 80 × 112 mm
Capacity: 3377 cc
Valves: Vertical overhead with pushrods
Induction: Carburettor

Wheelbase: 9 ft 6 in
Forward Speeds: 4 preselector
Front Suspension: Semi-elliptic leaf springs
Rear Suspension: Quarter-elliptic leaf springs
Chassis Frame: Channel-section
Maximum Speed: 110 mph

Talbot-Lago   France

Anthony Lago took over the French Talbot factory at Suresnes from the STD combine in the middle '30s and began building high-performance sporting cars. In 1938 his 4-litre sports cars, running stripped, competed in GP racing—outclassed, but competitors none the less. In 1939 he built a single-seater around the sports-car components, this car appearing in the French GP of that year, driven by Raymond Mays. The war over, this prototype single-seater Talbot-Lago was brought out again and developed, and in 1948 a series of improved cars was built.

They had box-section chassis frames, i.f.s. by transverse leaf spring and hollow upper wishbones, and a one-piece rear axle mounted on semi-elliptic leaf springs. The 6-cylinder engine with pushrod operated ohv from two camshafts mounted high in the block, was a full 4½-litre unsupercharged,

the limit of the Formula 1 of those days, and drove through a Wilson pre-selector gearbox. Behind this the transmission line was stepped to the right by a train of gears so that it ran alongside the driving seat to an offset differential assembly. These rugged cars were not outstandingly fast, but were reliable and economical, achieving 9 mpg.

The 4½-litre Talbot-Lagos were regular competitors in GP racing up to the end of 1951, when the Formula was abandoned, and though no major alterations were made to the general design of the car, details such as car-burettors, cylinder heads, brakes and horse-power figures were improved all the time. Early in 1951 Anthony Lago had to withdraw his works team, but private owners, headed by Louis Rosier, continued to race these large blue French cars. They were very tractable, Duncan Hamilton driving one across France when his transporter broke down. Some of the cars were converted into sports cars when they became obsolete for GP racing, and today most of the single-seaters still exist.

Year: 1948/51
Model: Monoplace Type 26C
Engine: Talbot-Lago
Number of cylinders: 6
Bore and Stroke: 93 × 110 mm
Capacity: 4485 cc
Valves: Inclined overhead operated by pushrods and rockers
Induction: Three carburettors

Wheelbase: 8 ft 2½ in
Forward Speeds: 4 pre-selector
Front Suspension: Independent by wishbones and transverse leaf spring
Rear Suspension: Rigid axle on semi-elliptic leaf springs
Chassis Frame: Box-section
Maximum Speed: 165 mph

Tecno

Italy

The brothers Luciano and Gianfranco Pederzani began by building vehicles for Kart racing in 1962, in their Bologna engineering factory. They progressed into the small racing-car scene, using proprietary engines, and really came to prominence in 1967 in International Formula 3 with their short-wheelbase, wide-track Tecno, which was very stable and handleable. It was natural to make the next step into Formula 2, using Ford engines and in 1971 they got the big chance that all racing-car constructors dream about. Count Gregorio Rossi di Montelera and his brother Vittorio, who control the giant drinks firm Martini, were looking for a project to sponsor under their Martini Racing banner, and visualized an Italian entry in Formula 1. They put a very large budget into the Tecno firm with the express desire to see a Martini-backed Formula 1 car in action.

Luciano and Gianfranco had just such an idea simmering, and in eighteen months they produced the first Formula 1 Tecno. They designed and built a flat-12-cylinder engine, not unlike the Ferrari of the time, and used a Hewland transmission, the whole package mounted in a tubular space-frame chassis with orthodox Formula 1 suspension. It was a bit of a hit-and-miss affair and by the time the first car appeared at the Belgian GP of 1972 it had undergone three major re-designs on chassis and suspension, and the flat-12 engine was changed from a seven- to a four-bearing crankshaft. The chassis was now an aluminium monocoque with tubular bracing, with the engine cantilevered out from the rear bulkhead of the cockpit and forming the rear half of the car. Nanni Galli drove this first car and at the end of the season he was joined by Derek Bell with a second version. Though the car showed promise on occasions it did not score any success, but everyone admired the ability of the Pederzanis to create their own raceworthy engine.

The following year saw the team in a confused state for while the engine building and development was done at the Bologna factory, the team management was British-based, and the finance was controlled from Turin. Not satisfied with the Italian chassis a young New Zealand mechanic, Alan McCall was brought in to design a new chassis and suspension. Before he completed the task he became disenchanted and left and the team tried to compete with the car, but lacked direction. An English designer, Gordon Fowell, then came on the scene with another new chassis design and the team became very disorientated, never knowing which path to pursue. For this season Chris Amon had been signed on as driver, and he too was soon confused. By mid-season the whole complicated affair blew to pieces and the Pederzanis slammed their doors and refused to let anyone have any more engines. Apart from the lack of direction over chassis design, the engine was not making any progress, for once it was working well, Luciano, the elder brother, who was the engine brilliance in the firm, lost interest and began designing a new engine, not wanting to do any more development work. This was a pity for the flat-12 engine had shown promise.

The internal fuss subsided and the team tried again, but soon foundered and by the end of the season it was all over and the Formula 1 Tecno was dead and buried. When the chassis disputes and complications were at their height, the Pederzanis suggested they threw the whole lot away and went back to Kart practice; that of using a flexible tubular chassis frame with no suspension at all. The thought of a 3-litre 450-bhp Kart did not inspire the drivers, or anyone else!

Year: 1967
Model: Formula 3
Engine: Ford
Number of cylinders: 4
Bore and Stroke: 80·1 × 48·4 mm
Capacity: 997 cc
Valves: Overhead, pushrod
Induction: Carburettor
Wheelbase: 6 ft 10¼ in

Forward Speeds: 4 Hewland
Front Suspension: Independent by double wishbones and coil springs
Rear Suspension: Independent by transverse links, radius rods and coil springs
Chassis Frame: Tubular space-frame
Maximum Speed: 130 mph

Year: 1972
Model: PA 123 F1
Engine: Pederzani
Number of cylinders: 12 horizontally-opposed
Bore and Stroke: 80·98 × 48·46 mm
Capacity: 2995 cc
Valves: Inclined overhead with two camshafts per bank
Induction: Lucas fuel-injection
Wheelbase: 8 ft 1¼ in (2470 mm)
Forward Speeds: 5 Hewland FG400

Front Suspension: Independent by double wishbones and inboard coil springs
Rear Suspension: Independent by single transverse top link, reversed lower wishbone, double radius rods and coil springs
Chassis Frame: Aluminium monocoque
Maximum Speed: 180 mph

The Tecno PA123 on the occasion of its presentation to the Press before the 1972 season

Tec-Mec   Italy

When Maserati withdrew from GP racing in 1958 plans were already advanced for a lighter and smaller version of the $2\frac{1}{2}$-litre 250F model. Designer Valerio Colotti took these plans with him when he left Maserati and formed a private firm known as Studio Tecnica Meccanica, or Tec-Mec for short. Some Modena enthusiasts persuaded him to go ahead with the special 250F, so he finished the design and handed the project over to the rest of the syndicate.

An engine and gearbox from an early 250F Maserati were installed in the Colotti chassis frame, with its all-independent suspension by means of wishbones and coil springs at the front, and wishbones and leaf spring at the rear. Money was limited and progress slow and, though the car could often be seen 'on test' at the Modena Autodrome, it was a long time getting to the starting line. Eventually it started in the 1959 United States GP, still with its second-hand engine, but it was outdated and far from raceworthy.

The Tec-Mec racing-car company was a separate entity from Studio Tec-Mec, and they built another car which consisted of an old 250F Maserati chassis, into which was fitted a Chevrolet Corvette engine, the idea being to race it in *Formule Libre* events in Australia. It was an unmanageable beast and expired quietly without causing much of a stir. The remains of this monstrosity were recently brought to England and rebuilt into a 250F Maserati. The Tec-Mec proper remained in America but was not raced, and came to England when Tom Wheatcroft bought it. After running it in VSCC Historic events for a short while it was put into the Donington Park Racing Car Museum, where it now languishes alongside a normal 250F Maserati, from which it was derived.

Year: 1959
Model: F415
Engine: Maserati 250F
Number of cylinders: 6
Bore and Stroke: 84 × 75 mm
Capacity: 2494 cc
Valves: Inclined overhead with
two ohcs
Induction: Three double-choke
Weber carburettors

Wheelbase: 7 ft 4½ in
Forward Speeds: 5
Front Suspension: Independent by
double wishbones and coil springs
Rear Suspension: Independent by
wishbones and transverse leaf
spring
Chassis Frame: Tubular space-
frame
Maximum Speed: Unknown

left The Tec-Mec Maserati 250F as it
is today in the Donington Park
Racing Car Museum

below Allan Staniforth in the
supercharged version of the Mark 1
Terrapin during his successful record
runs at Elvington airfield, Yorkshire

Terrapin England

Yorkshire-based enthusiasts Allan Staniforth and Richard Blackmore built
a sprint and hill-climb car in 1965 using BMC Mini components, which they
called the Terrapin-Min, having racked their brains for a bird, fish or animal
that had not been used before and would rhyme with Min. The car was so
successful that in 1968 Staniforth had an outing at a Records meeting and
annexed a number of records in the 1100-cc class at speeds around 130 mph.
He wrote a very detailed book about the car's design and construction and the
plans were offered for sale to anyone who wanted to build a similar car,

high speed and low cost being the keynote of the whole project. To date 44 cars have been built by private owners, while another 30 are under construction and the plans were sent as far afield as New Zealand and the West Indies.

The Mark 1 car was sold and Staniforth built the Mark 7 for his own use, the intervening Mark numbers being given to improved versions of the original car. The Mark 7, built in 1974, is still in regular use by the designer/constructor and differs principally in using rubber suspension in place of coil springs, though detail changes are continuous as with all home-built specials, for a one-off design is seldom completely finished.

Year: 1965
Model: Mark 1—record
Engine: BMC 'Mini-S'
Number of cylinders: 4
Bore and Stroke: 71·1 × 68·26 mm
Capacity: 1088 cc
Valves: Overhead with pushrods
Induction: Arnott supercharger
Wheelbase: 6 ft 8 in

Forward Speeds: 4
Front Suspension: Independent by wishbones and coil springs
Rear Suspension: Independent by wishbones and coil springs
Chassis Frame: Tubular space-frame with semi-stressed side sections
Maximum Speed: 140 mph

Thinwall Special

Anglo–Italian

Before starting the team of Vanwall cars the Vandervell Racing Team ran a series of Ferraris in the major racing events, learning a great deal about race organization as well as design and development. They were called 'Thin Wall Special' Ferraris, from the trade name of G.A. Vandervell's shell-bearings which were used by Ferrari and practically everyone else building engines. The first 'Thin Wall' was a 1949 short-chassis V12 supercharged 1½-litre Ferrari, and it was followed in 1950 by the brief loan of a two-stage supercharged, four ohc V12-cylinder 1½-litre 'works' Ferrari.

In 1951 Vandervell persuaded Ferrari to sell him one of the 1950 factory 4½-litre V12 unsupercharged cars, and from that point on the use of the name

Colin Vandervell in the rebuilt Thinwall Special on the occasion of its demonstration at Silverstone in 1973

Thin Wall Special became more and more justified, for the Vandervell Team modified the car extensively. By 1952 it had become the Thin Wall Special II, in as much that just about everything had been changed from the original car, engine, gearbox, chassis frame, bodywork, brakes as well as many of the engine internals such as pistons, valves, port shapes and so on. The Vandervell engineers were learning rapidly with all this development and much of the knowledge gained was going into the design of the first Vanwall Special. The Thin Wall Special was one of the first racing cars to use disc brakes successfully, the Vandervell firm making them in conjunction with Goodyear Aviation Division.

The result was an immensely powerful car, quite the equal of the factory 4½-litre Ferraris, and some idea of the potential of the 'Thin Wall Special' can be gained from the fact that such drivers as Farina, Taruffi, Hawthorn, Gonzalez and Collins all drove it with success. It raced regularly during the 1951/2/3 seasons, until the new Formula 1 started in 1954. Its 400 bhp battles against the V16 supercharged BRMs during 1952/3 still rank as classics. When the Vanwall Special got under way the Thin Wall Special was put out to grass.

It lingered in the Vandervell racing workshops for many years, neglected and forgotten, for the all-conquering Vanwall cars were the real pride and joy of the Acton factory. After Vandervell Products was bought by GKN following the untimely death of Tony Vandervell, the Thin Wall Special was completely rebuilt by the experimental department and made a re-appearance at Silverstone in 1973 to celebrate the twentieth anniversary of the year it set up the first 100-mph lap of the Silverstone circuit.

Year: 1953
Model: F1
Engine: Ferrari Tipo 375
Number of cylinders: 12 in-vee
Bore and Stroke: 80 × 74·5 mm
Capacity: 4495 cc
Valves: Inclined overhead with single camshaft per bank
Induction: Three four-choke Weber carburettors

Wheelbase: 8 ft 2½ in
Forward Speeds: 4
Front Suspension: Independent by double wishbones and transverse leaf spring
Rear Suspension: de Dion with transverse leaf spring
Chassis Frame: Tubular
Maximum Speed: 180 mph

Trojan   England

Trojan Engineering dates back to the early days of motoring, but the present firm has been involved in contract work for a long time. Their racing connections came through McLaren, as they built the production sports/racing

McLarens. By the time this activity ceased there was plenty of knowledge in the firm about modern racing-car construction and in 1972 Ron Tauranac joined the firm to lead the design of a Trojan F5000 car, the T102. This soon led to aspirations for Formula 1 and in 1974 the Trojan T103 appeared. It had many things in common with the F5000 chassis and used the conventional package of Cosworth DFV engine and Hewland gearbox in a monocoque chassis with orthodox suspension.

The brief appearance of a Trojan in Formula 1 racing was really nothing more than a wealthy businessman's dabble at the game, rather than a serious attempt to become a force in GP racing. The chairman of Trojan Ltd. Peter Agg, set a financial limit for this activity and it was just enough for one season. Tim Schenken drove the car and 1974 saw the coming and the going of the Formula 1 Trojan, but it left nothing in the way of a mark on the GP scene.

Year: 1974
Model: T103
Engine: Cosworth DFV
Number of cylinders: 8 in-vee
Bore and Stroke: 85·6 × 64·8 mm
Capacity: 2993 cc
Valves: 4 per cylinder, two ohcs per bank
Induction: Lucas fuel-injection
Wheelbase: 8 ft 6 in

Forward Speeds: 5 Hewland DG400
Front Suspension: Independent by double wishbones and coil springs
Rear Suspension: Independent by transverse links, radius rods and coil springs
Chassis Frame: Aluminium monocoque; engine a stressed member
Maximum Speed: 175 mph

Trossi-Monaco   Italy

This revolutionary machine was designed and built by Augusto Monaco and Giulio Aymini with Fiat support at first, but when they withdrew Count Trossi took over the financial burden and it was completed for the 1935 GP season. The chassis frame was made from small-diameter tubing on aircraft lines, in what we now call a space-frame, but in 1935 it was very unusual. On the nose of the fuselage was mounted a 4-litre 8-cylinder, double-piston 2 stroke engine, working on the split-single principle, air-cooled, with two Zoller Type M160 superchargers, and this drove the front wheels which were independently sprung. The driver sat very low inside the frame and the whole car was a new concept in racing. Unfortunately it was built at a time when the pace of technical development in GP racing was at a peak and there was little chance for a 'one-off' special to succeed.

It was constructed in the workshops at Count Trossi's palatial castle at Biella, in Northern Italy, and though it was tested at Monza it never raced. Today it lives in the Turin Automobile Museum.

---

left Tim Schenken in the Trojan T103 at the Spanish GP on the Jarama Autodrome in 1974

below The bizarre Trossi-Monaco on test at Monza in 1935 driven by Giulio Aymini

Year: 1935
Model: Monaco
Engine: Monaco-Aymini
Number of cylinders: 8 radial, double-piston
Bore and Stroke: 65 × 75 mm
Capacity: 3982 cc
Valves: None. 2-stroke
Induction: Zoller superchargers
Wheelbase: 7 ft 5¾ in (2280 mm)
Forward Speeds: 4
Front Suspension: Independent with lever-operated horizontal coil springs. Fwd
Rear Suspension: Independent with lever-operated horizontal coil springs
Chassis Frame: Tubular space-frame
Maximum Speed: 150 mph

Tyrrell
England

After running a Formula 1 team for *Engins Matra*, Ken Tyrrell embarked on his own project. With the assets of Jackie Stewart as his driver, and financial backing from Dunlop, Ford and the French ELF firm, he engaged Derek Gardner as his chief designer, and in great secrecy set him on the design of the first car to carry the name Tyrrell. This was in 1970, and while the car was being designed and built Tyrrell purchased a pair of March 701 cars to keep the team active. The new car was finished towards the end of of the season and was announced as the Tyrrell 001. It made its debut at the Gold Cup race at Oulton Park. Not a fairy-tale debut, as it gave trouble, but it did record fastest lap. It ran for the remainder of the season without success but provided plenty of useful information for winter development work.

Nineteen seventy-one saw Dunlop pulling out of Formula 1 and Tyrrell made a contract with Goodyear, while the ELF company backed his team wholeheartedly, so that the whole concern was called ELF Team Tyrrell. Francois Cevert joined the team and the second car was made 4 in longer in the cockpit to suit him, and also $1\frac{1}{2}$ in longer in the wheelbase, while the monocoque panels were made from 16-swg aluminium instead of the original 18 swg. This was 002 and, soon after, 003 appeared to the same specification. Whereas the original car had used a flat, wide lip ahead of the nose cowling, the new cars sported a full-width nose cowling, known as the 'bluff nose'. Experiments were carried out on 003 with special Girling twin-disc brakes, and a longer wheelbase was tried by the simple expedient of inserting a 4·3-in-long cast-alloy spacer between the Cosworth V8 engine and the Hewland gearbox, with longer mainshaft and radius rods to suit.

left Tyrrell 001, the first of a long line of successful cars, showing the wide nose 'blade' to create aerodynamic down-force on the front of the car

right Tyrrell 005 in its early form before the 'Trident' air-intake. Smooth air-flow round the cockpit and over the rear aerofoil was a prime objective

Victory came to the new Tyrrell marque in the 1971 Spanish GP at Barcelona, Stewart winning with 003. Later in the season Stewart and Cevert were 1st and 2nd in the French GP at Paul Ricard and other victories were scored in the German GP, the British GP, the Canadian GP and the United States GP. Before the end of the season a fourth car was built, 004, so that the two drivers were always well equipped.

In 1972 the team continued to be successful and a second series of cars was started with 005. This had a shorter wheelbase and was much 'quicker' in its actions, calling for the delicate touch of Stewart to get the best from it.

Having such a skilled driver leading the team Gardner was able to design a car that was almost beyond the capabilities of a lesser mortal, and to build into it a remarkable degree of 'swervability'. This new car started life with inboard-mounted front brakes, as well as inboard rear, but it was not long before the front ones were moved out to the hubs, mechanical problems not justifying the reduction in unsprung weight. The body contours were much flatter and more angular than on the earlier cars, and a lot of attention was given to air-flow over the body. A very tall air-collector box for the engine was used, obviously owing much to the tail intake on a Trident aircraft. By the end of the season a second Series II car 006 was built for Cevert. For 1973 006/2 was built for Stewart to the new specifications laid down in the Formula 1 rules, particularly with regard to the basic monocoque construction. Cevert's car 006 was written off in a crash in Canada in 1973 and 006/3 was hastily built only to be destroyed in a practice crash at Watkins Glen that killed the promising young French driver.

This blow, coupled with Stewart retiring, left the team in a very unsettled state and for the 1974 season Gardner designed the 007 Series III cars, somewhat 'detuned' in their handling so that the new drivers to the team would

not find them too difficult to adapt to. Jody Scheckter and Patrick Depailler were the new drivers and during 1974 and 1975 they used the 007 series cars, numbered 007/1 to 007/6, but the team was not as successful as in the heyday of Stewart and Cevert.

During the 1975 season Gardner was at work on an entirely new design that caused something of a furore when it was produced towards the end of the year, for it had six wheels! This was Project 34, the prototype being purely a research vehicle to prove the basic idea. The two main objectives were to reduce the front track and improve penetration through the air and

The 6-wheeled Tyrrell Project 34 in its first race form. This is number 2 in the P34 series

the design featured four tiny 10-in diameter front wheels replacing the more orthodox pair of 13-in wheels. Winter tests with the 6-wheeler proved conclusive and 1976 saw the team using Project 34/2, 34/3 and 34/4 and they were soon challenging all-comers. By mid-season Scheckter had notched up the team's first victory with this revolutionary design, finishing the season in 3rd place in the Manufacturers' Championship, and encouraging ELF Team Tyrrell to continue with the 6-wheeler concept in 1977.

Three cars, 34/5, 34/6 and 34/7 were built for 1977 with a new smooth one-piece bodywork, but the cars suffered from too much weight and a diminution of tyre development for the 10-in front covers, and they could not keep pace with new designs from Lotus and McLaren, even though Ronnie Peterson had replaced Scheckter at the wheel. At the end of the season Gardner left the Tyrrell team, where he had been for eight seasons, and his place was taken by Maurice Phillippe who produced a more conventional 4-wheeled Tyrrell, taking the serial number 008.

Year: 1970
Model: 001
Engine: Cosworth DFV
Number of cylinders: 8 in-vee
Bore and Stroke: 85·6 × 64·8 mm
Capacity: 2993 cc
Valves: Four per cylinder, two ohcs per bank
Induction: Lucas fuel-injection
Wheelbase: 7 ft 10¼ in

Forward Speeds: 5 Hewland
Front Suspension: Independent by double wishbones and coil springs
Rear Suspension: Independent by single top link, twin lower links, radius rods and coil springs
Chassis Frame: Aluminium monocoque; engine a stressed member
Maximum Speed: 175 mph

Year: 1976
Model: P34
Engine: Cosworth DFV
Number of cylinders: 8 in-vee
Bore and Stroke: 85·6 × 64·8 mm
Capacity: 2993 cc
Valves: Four per cylinder, two ohcs
per bank
Induction: Lucas fuel-injection
Wheelbase: To front axle 8 ft 4⅞ in;
to centre axle 6 ft 10⅝ in

Forward Speeds: 5 Hewland
Front Suspension: Independent by
double wishbones and coil springs
Rear Suspension: Independent by
single top link, twin lower links,
radius rods and coil springs
Chassis Frame: Aluminium
monocoque; engine a stressed
member
Maximum Speed: 180 mph

Vale Special

England

Manufacturers of small sv Triumph-engined sports cars, the Vale Company
of Maida Vale in London, built a special single-seater racing car for Ian
Connell in 1935. The chassis was basically a production one, of the underslung type, but the engine was a special Coventry-Climax 1½-litre with i.o.e.
valve arrangement, and was fitted with a large Centric supercharger, developing 97 bhp at 5700 rpm. Steering was unusual in having separate drag links
to each front wheel and no track rod. Suspension was non-independent and
the front axle was tubular. Replicas were offered at £625, but only the one
car was built, Connell racing it at Donington Park and Brooklands.

The supercharged Vale Special at the Brighton Speed Trials in 1935 driven by
Alan Gaspar

Year: 1935
Model: Single-seater
Engine: Coventry-Climax
Bore and Stroke: 69 × 100 mm
Capacity: 1496 cc
Valves: Pushrod overhead inlet,
side exhaust

Induction: Centric supercharger
Wheelbase: 7 ft 0 in
Forward Speeds: 4
Front and Rear Suspension:
Semi-elliptic leaf springs, underslung
Chassis Frame: Channel-section
Maximum Speed: 125 mph

Vanwall England

Motor racing was a hobby to Mr. G.A. Vandervell, owner of the VP Bearing empire, and after leaving the BRM project in 1949 he formed his own Vandervell Racing Team, operating various Ferraris. His aim was to build his own racing car and, above all else, to beat the Italians. The first Vanwall Special appeared in 1954, as a 2-litre 4-cylinder two-ohc car, after the general style of a Ferrari as far as the suspension was concerned, but with a Cooper-designed chassis frame. The engine was built entirely by Vandervell Products, with help from the Norton racing department. The name Vanwall was derived from Vandervell and Thinwall, the trade name of the VP engine bearings.

The classic Vanwall GP car of 1958 with wire-spoke front wheels and cast-alloy rear wheels

In 1955 the 'Special' part of the name was dropped and a team of cars was built called Vanwalls. After some ups and downs in 1956 the cars were completely redesigned with the help of Colin Chapman, and the team began to make very definite progress towards the ultimate goal, the Manufacturers' Championship. The car had two big advantages over most rivals; Bosch fuel-injection, which was producing 285 bhp from the 4-cylinder engine, and superior Goodyear disc brakes. In 1957, with an entirely new chassis, suspension and bodywork, the Vanwall began to challenge the best of the opposition, and in a fascinating story of steady but continual progress the team forged on from small victories to big victories, culminating in the winning of the Manufacturers' Championship in 1958.

The Vanwall was the first British car to win a Grande Epreuve since Sunbeam in 1923, when Moss and Brooks won the 1957 British GP at Aintree. The 1958 Vanwall team of Moss, Brooks and Lewis-Evans was one of the best in GP racing that Britain has ever produced. These three drivers dominated most of the races that season, winning six out of nine World Championship events and concluded that fine year by completely trouncing Maserati and Ferrari.

Racing as a hobby had long since gone by the board for Tony Vandervell, it was now a hard and continual business and technical project, and he was not a young man, having been racing at Brooklands in the 1920s. At the end of 1958 he was forced to withdraw from GP racing rather than risk doing his health permanent injury, so he reduced his efforts to one single car for a few races. It was a pity that the mighty Vanwall team, the first to really trounce the 'foreign opposition', should be reduced to an occasional entry. In 1960 Vanwall installed one of their 4-cylinder engines in a rear-engined Lotus chassis, and in 1961 built their own rear-engined car for Inter-Continental Formula racing, but its appearances were brief and disappointing. The Vanwall at the height of its success set an excellent standard of engine design, engineering and manufacture, and as well as doing much to raise the reputation of British engineering, it started the complete domination of GP racing by British cars, which lasted for many years.

Year: 1958
Model: F1
Engine: Vandervell
Number of cylinders: 4
Bore and Stroke: 96 × 86 mm
Capacity: 2490 cc
Valves: Inclined overhead with two ohcs
Induction: Bosch fuel-injection

Wheelbase: 7 ft 6¼ in
Forward Speeds: 5
Front Suspension: Independent by wishbones and coil springs
Rear Suspension: de Dion with coil springs
Chassis Frame: Tubular space-frame
Maximum Speed: 175 mph

Vauxhall-Villiers   England

In the search for a more powerful car for sprints and hill-climbs. Raymond Mays took one of the 1922 TT Vauxhall 3-litre cars, with its very advanced twin-ohc 16-valve 4-cylinder Ricardo-designed engine, and with the technical assistance of Amherst Villiers made an extremely powerful machine. Villiers supercharged the engine, developing the basically sound design to give nearly 200 bhp in sprint form, while the chassis was strengthened, as was the transmission. On this car Mays experimented successfully with twin rear wheels for hill-climbs, in order to transmit the power and also reduce the tendency for the tail to slide.

From 1928 to 1933 the Vauxhall-Villiers, or Villiers-Supercharge as it was sometimes called, was a star turn at Shelsley Walsh and similar events, with Mays as the driver. Later it passed into other hands, and after a successful season in 1936 with S.E. Cummings, it changed hands again. The new owner tried to improve on Villiers' ideas and put the engine into a Type 54 Bugatti chassis (a car whose own engine had gone into the BHW Special), but the project was unsuccessful and the Vauxhall-Villiers as it appeared in its heyday ceased to exist. In recent years it has been completely rebuilt, with an original TT Vauxhall chassis, into the form in which it was run in 1929, and competes in VSCC events.

Year: 1928/33
Model: Villiers
Engine: Vauxhall
Number of cylinders: 4
Bore and Stroke: 85 × 132 mm
Capacity: 2996 cc
Valves: Inclined overhead with two ohcs

Induction: Villiers supercharger
Wheelbase: 8 ft 11 in
Forward Speeds: 4
Front and Rear Suspension: Semi-elliptic leaf-springs
Chassis Frame: Channel-section
Maximum Speed: 130 mph

Veritas   Germany

The Veritas was built by Ernst Loof, a pre-war BMW engineer, who started in business in 1947. He took 328 BMW sports-car components and built sports/racing cars, developing his own designs, but still keeping a certain BMW lineage.

Eventually Loof developed his own Veritas engine which was a logical follow-on of the 328 BMW unit, retaining the classical vertical inlet port layout, but with a single ohc instead of the cross-pushrods. The single-seater versions were known as the Veritas-Meteor and they ran in Formula 2 racing. The final version of the racing Veritas was far removed from BMW origins, with wishbone and torsion bars suspension, 5-speed gearbox and the ohc

6-cylinder engine, which was built for Loof by the Heinkel firm. In German national racing Veritas were driven by such drivers as Hermann Lang and Karl Kling.

The firm finally ended up in a small premises behind the grandstand at the Nurburgring, but with the advance of German industry the smaller firms could not keep pace and Loof closed down in 1953 and rejoined BMW as a development engineer. Sadly, he died of a brain tumour in 1956.

left Raymond Mays at Shelsley Walsh in 1933 in the Vauxhall-Villiers in its most potent form

right Hermann Lang in the factory Veritas in the Nurburgring paddock in 1950. This had the single-ohc 6-cylinder Veritas engine

Year: 1950
Model: Meteor
Engine: Veritas (Heinkel)
Number of cylinders: 6
Bore and Stroke: 75 × 75 mm
Capacity: 1988 cc
Valves: Inclined overhead with single ohc
Induction: Three downdraught Solex carburettors

Wheelbase: 8 ft 0 in
Forward Speeds: 5
Front and Rear Suspension: Independent by wishbones and torsion bars
Chassis Frame: Tubular
Maximum Speed: 140 mph

Watson

America

A.J. Watson was a builder of chassis frames for Indianapolis cars towards the end of the era of front-engined 'roadsters'. They were designed to take the 4-cylinder Meyer-Drake Offenhauser engine and, under various sponsors' names, Watson-built cars won the Indy 500 in 1959, 1960, 1962 and 1964. Watson specialized in track-racing cars and was the originator of many ideas, such as varying the suspension on one side of the car to take advantage of the bankings, as well as attention to frontal area by canting the engine over almost horizontal. He studied the effects of weight distribution and its results on high-speed cornering and built cars with 'unbalanced' or 'asymmetrical' weight distribution. It was a Watson-built car that won the Monza 500 Mile Race at over 166 mph.

With the coming of the 'funny-car' era, or mid-engined European-style racing cars to Indianapolis, Watson did not take long to adapt to designing cars to the new layout.

Year: 1961
Model: Indy 'Roadster'
Engine: Meyer-Drake Offenhauser
Number of cylinders: 4
Bore and Stroke: 102 × 114 mm
Capacity: 4123 cc
Valves: Inclined overhead with two ohcs
Induction: Hilborn fuel-injection

Wheelbase: 8 ft 0 in
Forward Speeds: 2
Front Suspension: Rigid beam axle on torsion bars
Rear Suspension: Rigid axle on torsion bars
Chassis Frame: Tubular spaceframe
Maximum Speed: 180 mph

Williams England

After trading in various racing cars and dabbling in F3 racing, Frank Williams entered a Brabham BT26 in Formula 1 for Piers Courage in 1969, and the following year struck up a deal with de Tomaso in Modena. The Modena firm built 'British Kit Cars' around the ubiquitous Cosworth DFV engine and Hewland gearbox and Frank ran these de Tomaso cars for the 1970 season. An accident at Zandvoort that caused the death of Piers Courage rather took the wind out of this project, and for 1971 Williams bought a March 711. Two years of running March cars taught him a lot about car construction, for spares from March Engineering were difficult and costly, so he set about making his own parts and this naturally led to the building of a complete car, using various 'free-lance' designers. Although the first Williams car was completed in 1972 the scheme did not really get under way until the following year. Selling the car to sponsors, whose name it was then called, enabled Frank Williams to continue in Formula 1 though without

left A.J. Foyt in the Watson-built, Offenhauser-powered, Sheraton-Thompson Special with which he won the Indianapolis 500 in 1964

right The 1974 Williams Formula 1 car powered by a Cosworth V8 engine and driven by Arturo Merzario, when it was called an Iso-Marlboro

any signal success, mostly due to being unable to attract top drivers. The first car was called a Politoys, and subsequent ones Iso-Marlboros, but they became Williams cars in 1975.

When the Hesketh team folded up at the end of 1975 Williams bought the undeveloped 308C and formed a partnership with Austro–Canadian Walter Wolf who provided the finance to attract Harvey Postlethwaite, the Hesketh designer. While the 308C acted as a prototype in 1976, Williams FW05 cars followed, always using the Cosworth DFV engine. For 1977 the team was reconstituted as Wolf Racing and Frank Williams went off on his own and ran a March 761 for the Belgium driver Patrick Neve. In 1978 Williams built his own car, which is where we came in.

Year: 1974
Model: IR/03
Engine: Cosworth DFV
Number of cylinders: 8 in-vee
Bore and Stroke: 85·6 × 64·8 mm
Capacity: 2993 cc
Valves: 4 per cylinder, two ohcs per bank
Induction: Lucas fuel-injection
Wheelbase: 8 ft 6 in

Forward Speeds: 5 Hewland
Front Suspension: Independent by wishbones and coil springs
Rear Suspension: Independent by transverse link, wishbone, twin radius rods and coil springs
Chassis Frame: Aluminium monocoque; engine a stressed member
Maximum Speed: 175 mph

Wolf

Austrian-born Walter Wolf, now a Canadian businessman, financed the Frank Williams racing team in 1976, but disatisfied with the results he brought about a complete reshuffle and founded Walter Wolf Racing. Retaining designer Harvey Postlethwaite he signed up Jody Scheckter to drive and persuaded Peter Warr to leave Lotus and run the reformed team.

A brand-new car was designed, called the Wolf, and the 1977 season opened with a story-book win in the first GP in Argentina. The success of the small team has been remarkable, with three GP victories, culminating in winning the Canadian GP. For the season Scheckter had three cars, WR1, WR2 and WR3 at his disposal, so that he had always been well equipped, with a car to race, a spare car at the circuit and a third at the factory being prepared for the next meeting, the changes being rung on the three identical cars to spread their life even across the 17 race season.

The Postlethwaite design followed conventional lines in general concepts, but aimed at an uncomplicated, clean and straightforward car. Using the standard Cosworth/Hewland mechanical package, with great stress on functional aerodynamics, and handling characteristics suited to Scheckter's personal driving style, great attention was paid to keeping the weight down without sacrificing strength. The end result spoke for itself in its victories and its constant ability to be among the front runners at all times.

right The rare supercharged 2-stroke Zoller car in 1934, looking very like a W25 Mercédès-Benz
below The Wolf WR1 on the occasion of its initial unveiling in London at the end of 1976. It was painted dark blue with a gold stripe and carried the Canadian flag

Year: 1977
Model: WR
Engine: Cosworth DFV
Number of Cylinders: 8 in-vee
Bore and Stroke: 85·6 × 64·8 mm
Capacity: 2993 cc
Valves: Four per cylinder with two ohcs per bank
Induction: Lucas fuel-injection
Wheelbase: 8 ft 2 in plus 5-in spacer if required

Forward Speeds: 5
Front Suspension: Double wishbones and coil springs
Rear Suspension: Transverse links, radius rods and coil springs
Chassis Frame: Aluminium monocoque; engine a stressed member
Maximum Speed: 180 mph

Zoller
Germany

This was a small supercharged 2-stroke-engined racing car of the mid-'30s that, cosmetically, was modelled on the 1934 Mercédès-Benz. It ran in German national events and did not appear outside its own country. Designed by Swiss-born Dr. Arnold Zoller, already a noted 2-stroke specialist and designer of superchargers, the 6-cylinder double-piston 1½-litre engine gave 160 bhp, but Zoller died in January 1935 and the car did not reach full development.

Year: 1934
Model: Voiturette
Engine: Zoller 2-stroke
Number of cylinders: 6 on the split-single principle
Bore and Stroke: 43 × 84 mm
Capacity: 1465 cc
Valves: none
Induction: Supercharged

Wheelbase: ft in
Forward Speeds: 4
Front Suspension: Independent by transverse leaf spring and lower wishbones
Rear Suspension: Independent by swing axles
Chassis Frame: Channel-section
Maximum Speed: Unknown